Praise for *Survive to Win*

"It was heartwarming to read and relive Bob Watson's success as a player, coach, and now as the general manager of the world champions. The story is well told, and Bob Watson is a credit not only to baseball but to society as well."

Tal Smith
President, Houston Astros

"Bob Watson rewards the reader with a story rich in baseball history. *Survive to Win* is a must-read for anyone who loves the game and who cares about the people who really make it work."

Ron Shapiro
Sports Agent and Lawyer

"I knew Bob Watson was an outstanding major-league hitter and top-notch general manager—even before he helped build the Yankees into world champions. But now I know about Bob's determination and character. He's a courageous guy, and this book proves it."

Jon Miller
Analyst, ESPN Sunday Night Baseball

"*Survive to Win* is a story about the journey along the path to a World Series championship by the architect of the 1996 New York Yankees. It is a story about one of the strongest leaders of our time."

Fran Pirozzolo, Ph.D.
Sports Psychologist, New York Yankees

SURVIVE TO WIN

SURVIVE TO WIN

BOB WATSON

Vice President & General Manager of the 1996
WORLD CHAMPION NEW YORK YANKEES

with RUSS PATE

A
JANET
THOMA
BOOK

THOMAS NELSON PUBLISHERS
Nashville • Atlanta • London • Vancouver
Printed in the United States of America

Published in Nashville, Tennessee, by Thomas Nelson, Inc.,
Publishers, and distributed in Canada by Word Communications, Ltd.,
Richmond, British Columbia.

The Bible version used in this publication is THE NEW KING JAMES
VERSION. Copyright © 1979, 1980, 1982, 1990 Thomas Nelson, Inc.,
Publishers.

Library of Congress Cataloging-in-Publication Data

Watson, Bob, 1946–
Survive to win : the inspiring story of one man who overcame incredible
odds and came out a champion / Bob Watson.
p.   cm.
ISBN 0-7852-7193-7 (hardcover)
1. Watson, Bob, 1946–   . Afro-American baseball managers—
United States—Biography. 3. New York Yankees (Baseball team)—History.
4. Afro-American baseball managers—Religious life—United States.
I. Title.
GV865.W365A3 1997
796.357′092—dc21
[B]   97-10200
CIP

Printed in the United States of America.

1   2   3   4   5   6 — 02   01   00   99   98   97

For Carol, Keith, and Kelley—with all my love.

CONTENTS

ACKNOWLEDGMENTS

I would like to express my appreciation to Scott Waxman of the Literary Group, New York, and Janet Thoma of Thomas Nelson Publishers for their support and encouragement in turning the dream of this book into a reality.

I'd also like to extend a special salute to my wife, Carol Le'fer Watson, who compiled much of the background information for this book. Carol has been a source of strength and inspiration throughout my career in baseball. She has meant more to me than I've ever been able to express.

Thanks to my collaborator, Dallas-based author Russ Pate, for answering the call and working overtime. And to Dr. Fran Pirozzolo of Houston and Monica Reeves of Dallas for their contributions in developing and shaping the manuscript.

I am grateful for every mentor and friend who helped me grow as a ballplayer: Tommy Williams, Phil Pote, and Chet Brewer, the men who got me started in the game back in Los Angeles; Karl Kuehl, who signed me to a free-agent contract with the Houston Astros; Tommy Davis, who gave me an education in the art of hitting; Joe Torre, Don Zimmer, and Tony La Russa, who taught me bench strategy.

These acknowledgments would be incomplete without John McMullen and Bill Wood, who gave me a front office job with Houston in 1988; Drayton McLane, who named me as the first African-American general manager (GM) in baseball history in 1993; and George Steinbrenner, who brought me to the New York Yankees for the 1996 season and gave me the opportunity to be part of a world championship team.

I thank you one and all.

INTRODUCTION

I t's a long way from the Green Meadows playground in South Central Los Angeles to famed
Yankee Stadium in the Bronx—especially when you go by
way of a snake-infested swamp in Cocoa, Florida, and
several racially segregated towns below the Mason-Dixon
line.

A kid could easily make a wrong turn and get lost,
especially if he didn't have his bearings in life.

Come along on a journey from a dusty sandlot where
an eight-year-old boy hit a spellbinding home run all the
way to the final pitch in the 1996 World Series in front of
a jubilant crowd of New York Yankees fans.

The story I have to share is one of perseverance. It's a
story about overcoming the odds and steeling yourself
with an inner strength that can stare down adversity. It's
a story about building a foundation of faith that will sus-
tain a person through tough times—perhaps none
tougher than when cancer attacks and life is at risk.

This is also a story of preparation and dedication. I

was a good, solid major-league player for many years, though by no means a superstar. I have enjoyed several moments in the spotlight, such as when I scored baseball's one-millionth run in 1975 and when I became baseball's first African-American GM in 1993. And, of course, when the New York Yankees won the World Series last fall and I got to accept the World Series trophy in front of a huge national television audience.

This is also a story about finding your gift in life. The Lord makes each of his creations unique and gives each of us a special gift. Many people fail to recognize their gifts. Some reject the gift, tossing it away as a child discards an old toy. Fortunate souls are those able to identify and embrace their gift, because that embrace enables them to go as far as they can here on earth.

At its core, this book is about being true to yourself, about the process of self-discipline required to give supreme effort, and about learning how to win.

Baseball has been my life's work, and it has rewarded me far beyond my hopes and dreams. If this book inspires baseball fans to seek their gifts and follow their dreams, I'll be extremely pleased.

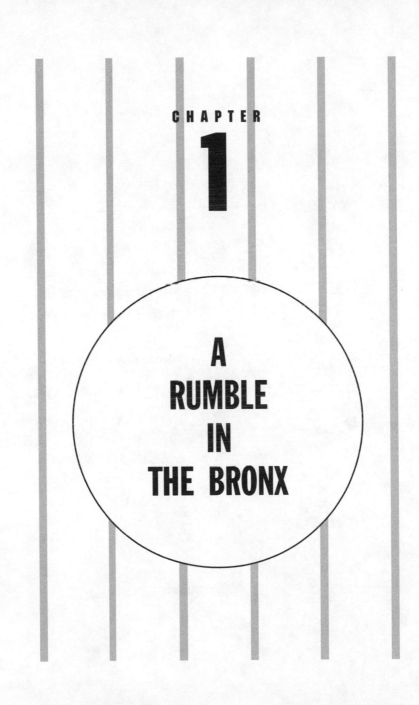

A
RUMBLE
IN
THE BRONX

At 10:56 P.M. on Saturday, October 26, 1996, with a capacity crowd of 56,375 at Yankee Stadium roaring on every pitch and millions of baseball fans around the world watching live on television, New York relief ace John Wetteland fired a 3-2 fastball on the outside corner to Atlanta second baseman Mark Lemke.

Lemke, a veteran second baseman who routinely elevates his performance in the postseason, was not the kind of pesky contact hitter Wetteland relished facing in a taut World Series game six. Not when Wetteland was trying to protect New York's 3-2 lead with two out in the top of the ninth inning and the tying run in scoring position. Not with the World Series outcome hanging in the balance.

But Lemke could not catch up with Wetteland's high-90s heat. The Atlanta veteran's reply was a soft pop foul, lifted lazily down the third-base line toward the ground-level seats. There waited New York's Charlie Hayes, one of a number of unheralded Yankees bench players whom circumstances had pressed into a starting role during the 1996 play-offs.

Hayes, a late-season acquisition from Pittsburgh (who

began platooning at third base when starter Wade Boggs injured his back) responded to the opportunity like a true professional. He didn't blink.

As if in slow motion, the white horsehide slowly descended out of the black of night and disappeared into Hayes's outstretched glove. He squeezed the ball securely and raised his glove skyward in an exultant gesture of triumph.

Hayes's catch set off a wild celebration. Yankees players and field staff, including first-year skipper Joe Torre and his trusty sidekick Don Zimmer, poured out of the dugout and raced toward the pitcher's mound to swarm Wetteland, whose brilliant relief pitching—saves in each of New York's four wins, a 2.08 ERA—earned him the coveted World Series MVP award.

The devout Wetteland barely had time for a thankful genuflection and quick gaze toward heaven before being buried in a dogpile near the mound. The cumulative weight of players and coaches nearly crushed his ankle.

Yankees fans, meanwhile, were hugging, kissing, exchanging high fives, and pounding each other on the back. The scene brought to mind the exuberance on Wall Street when the Dow-Jones average shot through the 6,000 barrier and kept climbing or Times Square at the stroke of midnight on New Year's Eve.

Yankee Stadium hummed with a mixture of jubilation, pandemonium, and undiluted joy. The mood was electric, something reserved for superhuman occasions like Pavarotti at the Metropolitan Opera or Sinatra at Carnegie Hall or Ali and Frazier at Madison Square Garden.

This was a magical moment in New York sports history, frozen in time and memory. Twenty years hence, Yankees fans will be able to say exactly where they were and what they were doing when Wetteland coaxed a pop-up from Lemke.

The din reverberating inside Yankee Stadium spilled over into the surrounding neighborhoods. There was a rumble in the Bronx, not some surrealistic staging for *West Side Story*, but a rumble representing the revelry associated with a world championship.

New York had won the World Series for a record twenty-third time, more than twice as many times as any other team in major-league history. The proud franchise, which has given the sports world such memorable figures as Babe Ruth, Lou Gehrig, Joe DiMaggio, Mickey Mantle, Yogi Berra, and Reggie Jackson, had earned its first world championship since consecutive pin-striped titles in 1977 and 1978.

An agonizing wait of nearly two decades—which, given the New York mentality of get-it-done-yesterday, seemed more like an eternity—was over. Uncork the champagne. Light the cigars. It's party time!

New York, which finished the 1996 season at 92-70,

four games ahead of Baltimore and seven up on Boston in the American League's Eastern Division, didn't waltz to a world title. The players, coaches, and front office personnel had to endure injuries, hotly debated trades and acquisitions, the usual assortment of slumps and funks, the microscopic examinations by the media, the fickleness of fans jumping on and off the team's bandwagon, and distractions from an assortment of personal and family matters.

During the 1996 play-offs, the Yankees had to survive tough showdowns, with first Texas and then Baltimore, before facing Atlanta, the defending world champion, in the World Series. Then the Yankees had to rebound from an immediate 2-0 deficit after they lost the opening two games at Yankee Stadium.

When the team left for Atlanta and games three through five at Fulton County Stadium, many of the most die-hard Yankees fans weren't expecting the World Series to return to the Big Apple.

Those fans were wrong. New York swept the three games in Georgia—rallying from a 6-0 deficit in game four to earn an 8-6 win in ten innings that turned the tide. The Yankees fans' emotions after Wetteland retired Lemke for the final out shook the city.

If I choose survival as the dominant theme for New York's 1996 season, that's because the concept hits especially close to home. In 1996, I survived my first season in the Yankees front office. At several critical junctures, I wasn't sure I would. Nor were the New York media, who speculated about how long I would last.

Although 1996 ultimately proved to be the most rewarding year of my three decades in baseball, a year marked by personal growth and enlightenment, it also presented no small amount of challenge, controversy, and obstacles.

Fifty-two weeks before the sixth and final game of the 1996 World Series—367 days, to be exact—I agreed to a two-year contract (with an additional two-year option) to take over as general manager of baseball's most closely watched team.

Lionized by some, loathed by others, the New York Yankees are one of America's few professional sports franchises with a national and international following. Long before anyone at NFL Films thought up the tag and pinned it on the Dallas Cowboys, the New York Yankees were the original "America's Team."

As a player for the Yankees in 1980 and 1981, and briefly in 1982, I knew firsthand the fishbowl experience of being a ballplayer in New York—having to perform in a pressurized environment where every move is magnified and inspected.

I made many mistakes, not the least of which was underestimating the extent to which front office personnel, like the GM, are under the same overzealous scrutiny and pressure as the guys wearing pin-striped uniforms.

I had never expected the Yankees GM post to become available during the fall of 1995, and I didn't expect New York's ownership to look to me to fill the position. I already had a good job—general manager of the Houston Astros—and was barely two years into a program to rebuild that franchise into a National League contender. Given a nucleus of young all-stars like Jeff Bagwell and Craig Biggio, and a bright young manager in Terry Collins, we were having fun, winning games, and emerging as a real force. As they say, life was good.

When the 1995 World Series between Atlanta and Cleveland began in the Georgia capital, Terry and I flew over to do some networking with other baseball people and put out feelers about possible trades. We balked, however, at the idea of following the series up north to Ohio. I knew night baseball in Cleveland at that time of year would be too cold for my blood.

On our return to Houston after game two, I was immediately notified that I'd received urgent phone messages from Drayton McLane, the Astros owner; Tal Smith, the Astros president; and Joe Molloy, general partner of the New York Yankees. Putting two and two together, I figured something significant, like a trade, must be brewing. And, if trade discussions were taking place at that level, above the GM, big names were being tossed around.

A big deal was in the works all right, but it didn't involve any players. I spoke first with Drayton who told me that he'd received a phone call from New York owner George Steinbrenner, asking permission to talk to me about the Yankees GM job. Drayton said Gene "Stick" Michael, the longtime organization man who had been everything from player and scout to manager and GM (Stick had been in the last position for the past five years), was being moved over to director of major-league scouting.

Drayton said he had given his okay to allow the Yankees to talk to me about the job and indicated that Joe Molloy, who is George Steinbrenner's son-in-law and who handles many of the day-to-day operations for the team, would be contacting me shortly to set up an interview. Drayton had one special request: that I call him back before making any decision to take the New York job. I assumed that he might be contemplating the possibility of making a counteroffer.

I next called Tal Smith, whom I've known for thirty-plus years, as far back as my first training camp with Houston in 1965, and who's been a mentor to me through all these years. Tal, who served as executive vice president of the Yankees in the mid-1970s and was familiar with the inner workings of the team's front office, told me he knew about New York's interest in my services and volunteered several questions to which I should seek answers.

Tal also advised me to be up-front in any conversations: "Bob, just tell them what you want, find out what they want, and then see what happens."

I thanked Tal for his counsel and support, then hung up. Next I placed a call to Joe Molloy, who works out of the Yankees business complex in Tampa, Florida.

Calling Joe was a no-brainer. Whenever people want to talk to you about anything—as long as it's legal, legitimate, and won't hurt anybody—it's in your best interest to hear them out. You should never erect walls between yourself and opportunity.

Adding another dimension to the circumstances, though, was the fact that for several months, Drayton McLane had been engaged in negotiations to find a new buyer for the Houston franchise. This meant, obviously, that my continued employment in the Astros front office was contingent on how soon, or if, Drayton made a deal.

I reached Molloy in his office at around 1:15 P.M. Houston time. We talked casually for a few minutes, and then he brought in Gene Michael, put on the speaker phone, and for the next few hours the three of us talked about baseball and about the Yankees job.

We discussed subjects like my philosophy about how to play the game, my style of leadership, and what I felt about winning. I made it clear that I wanted to have the resources necessary to be able to put together a winning team, as well as some semblance of job security.

Both Joe and Gene emphasized that the Yankees wanted to win and that the team also wanted to make a smooth, positive transition from Gene as GM to his successor. I could tell from their tone that the opportunity was firming up.

By late in the afternoon, around 5 P.M., I told Joe and Gene I needed to take a break. I was eager to call my wife, Carol, who was traveling abroad, and get her input on this rapidly escalating situation.

Carol, who is an accomplished artist, was part of a fashion study group on a tour of art museums and fashion galleries in Italy. When I reached her at a hotel in Florence, I asked, "Are you sitting down?"

"As a matter of fact, I'm lying down," she said sleepily. "I've had a long day, and it's after midnight. Why do you want to know if I'm sitting down?"

"I have a big-time question to ask you. I've been talking with the Yankees for the past few hours about a job as their vice president and GM. What do you think about that?"

There was silence at the other end of the line. Then Carol started humming a tune into the receiver. It sounded suspiciously like "I Love New York."

Daaaa-da-da-daah.

"Run," Carol finally said.

"Come again?"

"Run, run, run, Bob," she repeated. "It's an opportunity you can't turn down. Run and get it."

"Carol, do you *really* want me to take this job?"

"Yes," she replied. "There's a couple of things you have to consider. One, it's the most prestigious sports franchise in the world. I've seen people walking around here in Italy wearing Yankees caps. Let me tell you, I haven't seen one person wearing an Astros cap. The other thing you have to look at is the Yankees' winning tradition."

"I know," I said. "That's why I've been talking to them all afternoon."

Carol asked me point-blank if I was prepared to deal with the volatility in the Yankees front office, especially the owner's track record for firing staff (GMs and managers, in particular).

We discussed the contract terms Joe had mentioned: two years guaranteed, with two one-year options (*their* option, not mine) after that. I told Carol the offer on the table represented a nice raise over my salary in Houston, though it was more of a healthy increase than a windfall.

"Okay, we're really going to do this, aren't we, Bob?"

"Yes, we are," I agreed.

After saying good-bye to Carol, I held the phone in my fist and reflected on the magnitude of what was unfolding that afternoon. Here I was, a guy from inner-city Los Angeles, suddenly being offered the keys to the "House That Ruth Built"—the famed Yankee Stadium.

For an African American to sit in the GM's chair for the New York Yankees, the apex of baseball, represented a great moment not only for me personally but for minorities in general. If I could demonstrate the perseverance needed to reach the upper echelon of baseball management, they could too. Blacks, Hispanics, Latinos, women—minorities in baseball would now have something at which to aim.

I had been able to shatter the glass ceiling in baseball on October 5, 1993, becoming baseball's first African-American GM, with the Astros. Now on October 23, 1995, just two years and two weeks later, I was being asked to take the GM job in New York. I was being given the chance to mark a trail for generations of minorities yet to come.

I dialed McLane's number again and told him the Yankees were going to extend an offer and that Carol and I were prepared to accept. Rather than make a counteroffer or question my decision, Drayton gave me his blessing. He said he was pleased the New York opportunity was something my family and I wished to pursue. He wasn't about to stand in our way.

Yet I felt more than a little ambivalence about leaving the Houston franchise. I owed those people a great deal.

The Astros had signed me out of junior college and developed me into a major-league player. In 1988, Houston brought me into baseball administration as the first African-American assistant GM. Believe me, after all the Houston franchise had done for me and my family, the Astros would always have a special place in my heart.

But the opportunity to go to the Big Apple was, to borrow a line from Mario Puzo, an offer I couldn't refuse. I called Joe Molloy and Gene Michael back immediately and told them to call off the search; they had their new GM.

From the time I agreed to terms with the Yankees, my new boss made the mission statement clear:

"We want to win," George Steinbrenner told me. "I'll give you all the resources to do the job, Bob, but winning is the bottom line around here. We want a world championship as soon as possible. Preferably in 1996."

With Charlie Hayes's catch of Mark Lemke's pop fly, the mission had been accomplished exactly 367 days after I signed on. By George, we'd done it!

YANKEES VICTORY

Along with everyone else in the stadium, I was on my feet for every pitch in that incredible, electric ninth inning. Carol and I were in the GM's box, which overlooks the third-base side of home plate, along with Joe Molloy, Reggie Jackson, Mark Newman, who runs our minor-league operations and scouting, and Hal Steinbrenner, George's son and a general partner.

When Hayes grabbed Lemke's pop-up, I gave Carol a big bear hug. We were bouncing up and down in joy, just like kids on Christmas morning. I was overjoyed to share such an incredible moment with the special lady who for so many years has given me strength and inspiration.

I knew full well that without Carol's many sacrifices throughout the years, we wouldn't be where we were that night, which, let me tell you, felt like being above the clouds and on top of the world.

"I told you we were going to win four straight games," she said, harking back to a dream she'd had before the series began.

"Yeah, you did." I laughed. "But how come you forgot to say anything about those first two games?"

Both of us were crying. Big, wet, sticky tears of joy. I looked over at Joe Molloy and saw that he was crying too. Down on the field, where the players had formed a dogpile, hundreds of police officers, some of them mounted on horseback, were lining the field, keeping fans from running out of the stands. The fans, though, were too busy going bananas to storm the field.

Yankees players suddenly wiggled free from the scrum on the mound and began a spontaneous victory lap, expressing their gratitude to the frenzied fans and ratcheting up the decibel level inside the stadium. One lasting image from the celebration on the field was the sight of Wade Boggs riding horseback behind a mounted policeman, the index finger of Wade's left hand held aloft to signify that "We're number one."

I recall Yankees legend Reggie Jackson, who's now a special adviser to the team, pounding me on the back. "We did it!" Reggie shouted. "We did it! We did it!" Then Yankees scouts like Ron Brand, Ron Hanson, Chuck Cottier, and Wade Taylor; our international scout, Gordon Blakeley; and Billy Connors, our pitching coordinator, started pouring into the box to offer their congratulations. Next came David Sussman, our executive vice president and general counsel, and Barry Pincus, the chief financial officer.

I pulled out a handkerchief and tried to stop the tears, which were dripping like a faucet. I never did let go of Carol, however. My legs felt wobbly, and butterflies were churning in my stomach. I clung to her for support.

Someone from the PR staff came in and said I was needed down in the clubhouse for the presentation of the World Series trophy. I steadied myself, took a few deep breaths, and gathered my wits to go face the mass of humanity I knew waited there. I told Carol to stay upstairs to celebrate. I'd see her later.

By the time I reached the clubhouse, champagne was

flowing freely. Players were donning world championship T-shirts and caps, and I couldn't wait to perform
this and every other ritual (like lighting up a victory ci-
gar) of a championship locker room.

I began hugging players, coaches, and staff, slowly
making my way around a crowded clubhouse designed
for forty players but filled with literally hundreds of
beaming Yankees fans, including actor Billy Crystal and
New York Mayor Rudy Giuliani.

Manager Joe Torre finally came in from the field and
we embraced. Joe and I didn't have to say a word to each
other; we knew what we'd endured to reach that point.
Words were superfluous for two guys who had grown as
close as brothers.

Then it was time for the presentation of the trophy,
which Joe and I accepted on behalf of the Yankees from
Bud Selig, baseball's acting commissioner. All I can remember about that moment is saying something about
how proud I was to be holding that trophy and pointing
out how heavy it was.

Then I congratulated the Steinbrenner family, Joe
Torre and his staff, and all the players. I looked directly
into the TV cameras and said how proud I was to be the
first and only African-American GM to win a world championship. I made note of the fact that Jackie Robinson
had broken the color line in baseball forty-nine years
earlier.

That evening, and over the course of the next few days, I took great satisfaction in reflecting on how much we had accomplished as an organization, top to bottom. From the moment I accepted the Yankees' offer, personnel decisions had been virtually nonstop. It underscored the fact that in baseball administration there never is any downtime. The job entails year-round duty, and frequently the "off-season" between the end of the World Series in October and the opening of spring training in February proves to be busier than the regular season.

BUILDING
A WINNING TEAM

In the hundred or so days between when I joined the Yankees in October 1995 and when we opened camp in Florida in February 1996, I had handled a series of transactions that shaped the destiny of the '96 team.

In November, we acquired catcher Joe Girardi from the Colorado Rockies for pitcher Mike DeJean and a player to be named. Girardi brought the defensive skills so important to success at the major-league level. I'm a big believer that defense in baseball starts up the middle—catcher, pitcher, second base, shortstop, and center field—and with Girardi, we would have a cornerstone. Plus, Joe was particularly adept at blocking balls in the dirt, where so many of today's pitchers throw their split-fingered "out" pitches. (Don Zimmer had pushed particularly hard for the acquisition of Girardi, and I'm glad he did. During the '96 season, Girardi hit .294, played great defense, and provided terrific leadership with a rock-steady approach that all his teammates admired.)

In December, we re-signed free agent Wade Boggs to a two-year contract; made a trade with Seattle that brought in Tino Martinez, Jeff Nelson, and Jim Mecir; and signed free agent Mariano Duncan, a veteran infielder who most recently had played at Cincinnati. We added Duncan for infield depth, but when Pat Kelly got injured in training camp, Mariano stepped into a regular role. It was Duncan who coined a motto for the 1996 New York Yankees: "We play today. We win today. Dassit."

In Boggs (third base), Martinez (first base, replacing Don Mattingly, who had announced he was going to sit out the '96 season), and Duncan (second base), we had the nucleus of the starting infield. And what a nucleus it proved to be, with both Duncan (.340) and Boggs (.311) hitting over .300 and Martinez leading the team with 117 RBI.

Late in the month we re-signed pitcher David Cone to a three-year contract, plus two option years, and acquired Tim "Rock" Raines in a deal with the Chicago White Sox. Cone and Raines would both battle back from injury and give the team a huge lift during the stretch drive in September. We also signed left-handed starting pitcher Kenny Rogers, formerly of the Texas Rangers, to a four-year contract at the end of January.

I sometimes compare the GM's job on a baseball team with that of an architect's. The GM principally creates the blueprint, or design for a team, and assembles the raw materials (players) required for that particular style. Then the architect turns things over to the construction superintendent (the field manager) and his foremen (coaches) who see that the project is carried out in accordance with the architect's vision.

Where the architectural analogy breaks down a bit, I suppose, is that a baseball GM never gets to see his masterwork, like an Empire State Building or Chrysler Building, actually completed. You never have the chance to relax, kick back, and admire your creation.

That's because a baseball team's roster changes constantly. Through trades, free agency, waivers, injuries, and whatever else occurs, players come and go. Rather than ever being a finished product, a baseball team represents a work in progress. GMs, therefore, are constantly evaluating talent, seeing what they need to add to (or subtract from) their ball club.

About the only major architectural decision concerning the '96 Yankees that I did not make involved Buck Showalter, the team's field manager in 1995. George

Steinbrenner and Joe Molloy handled that negotiation, which concluded on October 26, three days after I came aboard, and ended with Buck deciding not to return for the '96 season. (Showalter subsequently became manager of the new franchise in Arizona, which begins play in 1998.)

When George and Joe asked me to prepare a list of candidates to replace Buck, I had one prime candidate in mind: Joe Torre. Never mind that he had been fired as manager of the St. Louis Cardinals during the 1995 season or that his winning percentage in roughly 1,900 games as a manager was .471. Joe Torre was my guy.

My close association with Joe dated back to the final years of my active career; I played for him when he managed the Atlanta Braves. For a number of years before that, of course, I had played against him in the National League. We had spent a lot of time together talking about baseball, particularly hitting.

There were so many things to admire about Torre, but one quality I particularly liked was the fact he could deal with adversity. He had tasted the sweet nectar of success in baseball, having been a multitime all-star, as well as the National League's batting champion (.363) and MVP in 1971. He had also tasted the pits, having had a year with the New York Mets when he struggled at the plate and was hounded by boo-birds.

Joe had seen, as I like to say, both the penthouse and

the outhouse during his years in the major leagues. Because of those experiences, he possessed the patience to ride out the bumps that inevitably occur during such a long season (the '96 Yankees played more than two hundred games), including spring training games in March and the play-offs in October. I knew he wouldn't panic when fortune turned against us.

In retrospect, one of the major reasons the Yankees won the World Series in 1996 was the solid and consistent leadership provided by Joe and his field staff, which included bench coach Don Zimmer (another former skipper of mine with the Boston Red Sox), pitching coach Mel Stottlemyre (the former New York Yankees great whom I brought with me from Houston), hitting coach Chris Chambliss (a teammate of mine in Atlanta), outfield coach Jose Cardenal (one of the best defensive players of his era), infield coach Willie Randolph (a great ex-Yankee and former team captain), and bullpen coach Tony Cloninger (a 20-game winner during his major-league career).

Each of those men made huge contributions to our success. I could cite countless examples, but here's one memorable one: In the bottom of the ninth inning of game five of the World Series, with John Wetteland facing pinch hitter Luis Polonia with two out and two on, Jose Cardenal motioned to right fielder Paul O'Neill to move several steps toward center. On the next pitch,

Polonia hit a screamer toward the gap in right center, but O'Neill, despite an injured hamstring, tracked it down. After making the game-ending catch, Paul pounded the outfield wall in ecstasy.

If Jose had not made that one adjustment with our outfield defense, the Yankees would have lost the game 2-1 and come back from Atlanta trailing three games to two. Instead, we came home to the Bronx ahead by that same margin—and promptly took care of business.

Working together, Joe and his staff kept a steady hand on the tiller at all times. They weathered the storms that brewed up around the team as we headed into the homestretch of an unforgettable season.

CHAPTER

2

PICKING
YOUR
SPOTS

During New York's 1996 championship season, I addressed the team collectively three times: once at the outset of spring training camp to communicate the mission statement, once early in May to inform everyone about David Cone's aneurysm and surgery, and once during the World Series, before the start of game two, to encourage the players to believe in themselves and to battle Atlanta to the best of their ability.

Otherwise, I adhered closely to the organization's lines of communication and chain of command. Speaking directly to the team, except on special occasions or in special circumstances, isn't the job of a general manager. Or, at least in my opinion, it shouldn't be.

That's a job for the field staff—Joe Torre and his coaches. Their jobs involve interacting with players, teaching, and coaching on an everyday basis. One of the field staff's numerous responsibilities is keeping a finger on the pulse of what's going on inside the clubhouse. They are the ones who have to monitor how players are bonding and how the team is solidifying. Its chemistry, in other words.

I remember from my own playing days how much

tension a GM created when he started hanging around the clubhouse. *What's* he *doing down here?* players would immediately ask themselves. *What's in the works? Why is this guy poking his nose into our business?*

Mindful of that, I make it a policy to keep myself out of the Yankees clubhouse, respecting the sanctity of the players' space. I go so far as to always enter Joe's office from a side door, not the main one. When I have to go to the training room to check on an injured player, I generally take the long way around the clubhouse.

Consider for a moment that a baseball team is like the ingredients for a rich and hearty stew. The different personalities and characters on a twenty-five-man roster represent the meat, potatoes, onions, celery, and tomatoes that go into the recipe. But even with such tasty ingredients, somebody has to add the right amount of seasonings and spices to get the taste just right.

On a baseball team, that person is the field manager. He's the master chef, and his coaches are the assistant chefs. The point of this analogy is that you don't want too many chefs stirring up the pot. Not the GM. Not anyone else from the front office, either, including the team's top brass.

That's why, speaking of channels of communication and chains of command, I made a special request to George Steinbrenner from the outset of my tenure with the New York Yankees: If you have business to discuss with the manager, let me be the intermediary. Please come to me first; then I'll take the matter to the skipper. Don't go around me or leave me out of the loop.

For the same reason I don't deal directly with any of Joe's ballplayers, I don't believe an owner should deal directly with the manager. It's a management philosophy that I think should be adhered to and respected. (Speaking of respect, it's been my experience that the more respect each member of an organization extends toward everyone else, the better that organization will run.)

The manager of a major-league club has plenty to fill up his waking hours—the proverbial full plate. He doesn't need the additional responsibility of having to interact with a team's owner. That's not in a manager's job description, nor does it fit the chain of command. I've never believed that micromanagement is good for business.

George Steinbrenner, to his great credit, respected my request. To my knowledge, he called Joe directly only twice during the 1996 season: once in June, when Joe's brother Rocco passed away suddenly from a heart attack, and again in October, when Joe's brother Frank received his well-publicized heart transplant.

George kept his conversations with Joe strictly on a personal basis. He didn't, as he had been known to do at times, involve himself in the various layers of the team. He let me do my job as GM, and, in turn, I let Joe do his job as manager. That way, results could be attributed to the people doing their specific jobs. There's nothing novel or magical in an approach that allows people to be held accountable for their own performance, good or bad.

It's hard to know, when feedback is coming from all directions and adjustments are made on the basis of yesterday's box score, who is responsible for what. Imagine a hitter, who's battling a slump, having to listen to several different hitting instructors. They might all know their stuff and be earnest in applying the principles they believe in, but the inevitable result will be a totally confused, messed-up hitter who is lucky to bat a buck-fifty (.150).

The system we put in place minimized distractions. We let Joe and his assistants stir the pot and bring the stew to a boil. I wish I could describe how tasty the whole experience was for all of us on the evening of October 26, 1996, at Yankee Stadium. And how our fans cried out for more.

I've been asked many times during the current off-season what I consider the biggest single factor behind the Yankees world championship in 1996:

- Was it the routinely sensational play of rookie shortstop Derek Jeter, who most assuredly deserved his American League Rookie of the Year award?

- Was it the dominating performance of the bull pen, especially setup man Mariano Rivera and closer John

Wetteland? If other teams couldn't get us down early, thanks to those guys, the opposition had virtually no chance of beating us late. In 1996 the Yankees were a remarkable 75-3 in games we led after six innings and 86-1 when we led after eight. When we got teams in a hole, we buried them.

• Was it the emergence in the postseason of outfielder Bernie Williams, who stamped himself as one of the game's newest superstars? Williams carried the team through the first round of the play-offs against Texas, when he engaged in a slugging duel with one of his boyhood pals from Puerto Rico, Juan Gonzalez. Then he continued his rampage against Baltimore.

• Was it the breakthrough season for starting pitcher Andy Pettitte, who won 21 games and, in my opinion, deserved the Cy Young Award? Pettitte was a sterling 13-3 in games he pitched after a Yankees loss.

• Was it the team's overall depth? Was it the acquisition, during the season, of position players like Darryl Strawberry, Cecil Fielder, and Charlie Hayes, as well as pitchers David Weathers and Graeme Lloyd?

Actually, I believe we won because of all those things and much, much more. My response to the question about the biggest single factor behind our success is a simple one:

We had a clubhouse full of guys who put the team first. They checked their egos at the door and never let selfish, individual goals or moods interfere with team goals. In so doing, they followed the philosophy I had stressed way back at the beginning of spring training in my first address to them.

The team had assembled in mid-February 1996 at the Yankees complex in Tampa. The players had gathered in the locker room, where Joe Torre had just introduced his support staff and gone over some of the team rules during camp, when I decided to speak up.

"Gentlemen," I said, "if we're going to win a championship this year, and I think we have the potential right here in this room to do it, you're going to have to come together as a team.

"We have to focus on these three words: *we, us, team.* We're going to have to realize that success is not an individual thing but rather a collective accomplishment. Not one of us in here can win a World Series all by himself. I can't, Joe can't, none of us can. But working together, there are no limits to what the New York Yankees can accomplish—that is, if we keep a team-first, winning attitude and go about our business like champions."

The *we, us, team* motto, incidentally, wasn't anything original on my part. It's the same message my baseball coach, Phil Pote, stressed to his players at Fremont High School in Los Angeles back in the 1960s. I'm sure baseball coaches have been using variations of the same theme for the past century.

Why? Because it happens to be true. Teamwork makes a crucial difference in sports. It's a true standard of excellence, one that Pat Williams, executive vice president and former general manager of the NBA's Orlando Magic, discussed in an entire book.

I brought up the subject that day because I strongly believe that players on a team have to sacrifice for one another. Selfishness is a subtle disease that on many teams saps the will to win. It's like a hidden cancer.

The second point I made to the team in 1996 was that we were going to play percentage baseball. To encapsulate that philosophy into a pet phrase, we were going to "Get 'em on, move 'em along, get 'em in." We were going to play solid, fundamental, yet aggressive baseball. It's the way I believe the game should be played, and it fits with Joe Torre's managerial style: Be the intimidator, not the intimidated.

"Gentlemen, I'm going to expect each of you to concentrate on playing the 'inside' or 'hidden' game of baseball," I said. "We're going to concentrate on doing the little things that don't necessarily show up in the box score, like running the bases with your head up and watching your coaches for the signals. One of the worst things a team can do is surrender free outs by making mistakes on the base paths, but bad teams somehow do it all the time. Baserunning blunders cost a team more wins than people realize.

"Outfielders, we want you first and foremost to hit the cutoff man. We're not going to give away cheap extra bases. Pitchers, we want you to get ahead in the count. As good as major-league hitters are, if you consistently get them down in the count at 0-2 or 1-2, every last one of you has the potential to be another Sandy Koufax. Because when batters are down in the count, they hit something like .180. When hitters get the advantage in the count, they hit over .300.

"There's one other thing, guys. We're going to play twenty-seven outs a game, twenty-eight at the most. We're going to play as hard on the last out as the very first one. We're not going to be one of these ball clubs that give the other team twenty-nine or thirty outs to deal with. That's how you get yourself beat."

Those last words proved to be prophetic. When the Yankees rallied from the 6-0 deficit in game four of the World Series (our comeback keyed by Jim Leyritz's three-run homer off Mark Wohlers), the Braves had given us a couple of extra outs. In the sixth inning, after Derek Jeter's foul ball down the right-field line dropped in, he started our rally with a base hit; in the eighth inning, right before Leyritz's homer tied the game, the Braves failed to turn a key double play when Rafael Belliard misplayed a ground ball. Had the Braves made either of those plays, we probably would have faced a 3-1 deficit in the series. Instead, they gave us extra outs.

LESSONS FROM SPRING TRAINING

There are a couple of lessons you can draw from my remarks to the Yankees in spring training. One, I'm no Knute Rockne. The good Lord did not bless me with a natural flair for speaking, but he did allow me to develop a certain wisdom for recognizing how people behave on a team and how they can get the most out of themselves.

Not a single Yankees player who heard me felt motivated to jump up and run through either the clubhouse door or the nearest brick wall. But everything about their style of play in 1996 showed they were listening intently as I expressed my philosophy.

Another lesson I've learned through the years is that *doing the little things correctly* gives a team the opportunity to achieve bigger things. I don't believe you can achieve greatness in baseball, or any other endeavor, without paying attention to detail or without being prepared every day.

You have to do the little things that are seldom

recognized or talked about but, nevertheless, remain essential to the task. I have learned through experience that in a person's quest to achieve monumental things in life, he or she must never lose sight of the fundamentals. You can't take them for granted.

You also have to have people around you who share the vision and the philosophy of "doing things the right way." People who will relish a lot of small, and sometimes private, victories.

Another lesson I tried to convey to the team that day is that *success is a collaborative process*. No one in sports, especially in team sports, can become a champion without having a support system of managers, advisers, and trainers.

One of the most frequently heard statements in sports is "There is no 'I' in T-E-A-M." While that is trite but true, let me add a slightly different spin:

There is no "I" in S-U-C-C-E-S-S.

While success to any significant degree requires that a person be focused on a goal and committed to the task—and emotionally and spiritually prepared to persevere—success simply cannot occur within a vacuum.

Success is the product of preparation. That preparation necessarily involves the participation of many. No one gets anywhere in life without being taught, prepped, schooled, and mentored. Truly successful people in life remember and respect the many others who have helped them along the way.

In my own baseball career, I'm indebted to people like Phil Pote, Karl Kuehl, Tal Smith, and many other gentlemen I'll mention in this book. I'm not vain enough—or foolish enough—to think I got where I did by myself.

What's the big deal about the remarks I made to the New York players at spring training, you ask? Doesn't every one of the twenty-eight teams in the major leagues begin each spring training with the same sort of rah-rah, put-the-team-first type of speech?

You might be surprised to learn this, but it's not the norm. In my twenty-plus years at major-league training camps, I never heard a GM or, for that matter, a field manager lay out the team's philosophy and communicate its vision. Not once.

Maybe that's another example of the male of the species being noncommunicative or taking things for granted. Maybe people in positions of authority with baseball teams assume players understand that the object is to win games and conclude, therefore, that the subject doesn't need to be addressed.

Getting everyone on the same page is an important part of real leadership. Leadership is exemplified by defining a shared vision, communicating that vision, helping define individual tasks to accomplish the goal, and getting everyone involved, from the bottom up, to buy into the mission.

Leadership is more than calling all the shots. It's more than barking out orders. Leadership is about innovation, enthusiasm, and setting a tone by setting an example. Leadership is about listening and adjusting. Leadership is about being firm but fair, about knowing when to give people some rein and when to tug in on the reins. Leadership is also about following through.

THE SECOND ADDRESS

My second address to the club occurred in early May when David Cone, a few days after throwing a complete game in a 5-1 win over Chicago, was diagnosed with an aneurysm in his right shoulder. David had been experiencing circulation problems that affected his pitching hand, and now we knew the source of the problem. Our team physician, Dr. Stuart Hershon, immediately scheduled corrective surgery for David, because an aneurysm can be dangerous.

I gathered the team in the clubhouse and summarized my conversations with David and Dr. Hershon. "Gentlemen," I said, "I want to bring you up to speed on David Cone's condition. The problems he's been having are caused by an aneurysm in his shoulder. It's a serious condition, so we've scheduled him for surgery at once [May 10], but let me stress that we don't believe it is life-threatening.

"Our main consideration at this point is for David the human being. Not David the pitcher, not David your teammate. We're going to do whatever we can to give him and his family our total support.

"I probably should also tell you there's a good chance David won't be able to pitch again this year. And I think we all know what that means.

"There's no replacing a number one starter like David. But I want each of you guys on the [pitching] staff to step up and help carry the load. It's going to be a tough row to hoe, but I don't want any one guy to think he has to try and do more than he's capable of doing. I can also tell you from experience that a heavy load becomes lighter when it's shared. So let's pick each other up.

"And guys," I added, "there's one other thing. David asked me to ask you to say a prayer for him."

David Cone underwent successful surgery in mid-May (a vein graft was placed in the damaged artery in his shoulder), then spent seven weeks healing. He started a conditioning program in July and began throwing again in August. After a couple of starts at AA Norwich, he returned to the active roster.

On Labor Day in Oakland, with the Yankees' lead in

the American League East shriveled to four games, Cone capped a remarkable comeback by pitching seven innings of no-hit ball in his first action in exactly four months. His presence energized the team and steadied the starting rotation.

One of the pitchers who helped carry the load in Cone's absence was Dwight Gooden. Returning to baseball in 1996 after a lengthy suspension, Doc made his own statement about stepping up on May 14 against Seattle. Flashing the stuff that won him a Cy Young Award in the National League, Gooden no-hit the mighty Mariners at Yankee Stadium. Doc would win eleven games in 1996 and help fill the breach caused by Cone's injury.

THE FINAL ADDRESS

My third and final address to the team came before the second game of the World Series. We had been routed 12-1 in Game One, showing the rust from having to wait around while Atlanta and St. Louis settled the National League pennant.

I had purposely avoided taking part in team celebrations after the play-off series wins against Texas and Baltimore. But now I decided to step forward.

Basically, I thanked the Yankees players for the effort they had extended to win the American League pennant.

I lauded them for staying within the framework of putting the team first.

"Gentlemen," I said, "on behalf of management, I want to thank each of you for going about your business this year in the manner that you have. And there's something else I want you to know: Seven times in history, the Yankees have lost the first game of a World Series and then come back and won the world championship. I am confident that you're going to be the eighth Yankee team to do it.

"Forget about losing Game One. Play the rest of the series as you've played all year, and you'll be fine. Just relax, and go out and play Yankee baseball."

While I carefully pick my spots for addressing the ball club collectively, or the players individually, I do spend a great deal of time talking about the New York Yankees. In the role of GM, I serve as the team's official spokesperson with the media, which puts me in daily contact with beat writers, columnists, TV reporters, and anchors—you name it.

COMMUNICATING FOR THE YANKEES

Working with the media is one of the most essential roles for a baseball GM. The flow of information out of a ball club is critical for a team's marketing and image, and accessibility is a must. I probably spend, on average, a couple of hours a day handling queries from the press. During the season, I probably average forty phone calls a day. Sometimes fifty or more if news is breaking.

In New York, we have eight beat writers and even a radio reporter following the club every day, at home and on the road. Contrast that with the media coverage in Houston: When I took over as Astros GM at the end of 1993, there were two newspapers in town—the *Houston Post* and the *Houston Chronicle*. By the time I left for New York, there was only one. The *Post* had ceased operations.

In truth, media relations isn't my favorite part of the job. As I mentioned, I wasn't blessed with the gift for coming up with either the quick one-liner or the eloquent statement as, for example, a Joe Torre is. Nevertheless, talking with the media takes a big bite out of my workday.

When I'm not discharging those duties, I'm typically talking to other people within the organization. I talk daily with Mark Newman, who oversees our farm system from Tampa, going over the progress of players in the minor leagues. I also confer daily with our medical staff and trainers about the treatment and rehabilitation of injured players.

I'll talk with my immediate boss, Joe Molloy, about matters affecting the ball club. I'll talk with Joe Torre about how the team is going or maybe about an upcoming opponent. I also talk frequently with George Steinbrenner.

If I'm not on the telephone, I'm generally in a meeting. People engaged in ticket sales, corporate sponsorships, marketing, advertising, public relations, stadium operations, and concessions report directly to me. Within the organization we conduct all manner of planning, scheduling, and administrative duties.

My immediate staff consists of Brian Cashman, the assistant GM, Tom May and Gene Keohane in operations, David Szen, our traveling secretary, and Richard Cerrone, public relations director. I can't say enough about the way these men discharge their duties with great enthusiasm and professionalism. They bring a great esprit de corps to the office and do an exemplary job in handling all the information and paperwork that flow in and out of a major-league office. Believe me, their jobs can be logistical nightmares. They're winners, every one.

The Yankees are, in essence, a $130 million corporation. We have a player payroll of $66 million, the highest in baseball. Ours is a full-time, year-round job. Free time is anything left over after the fifteen- to eighteen-hour workdays during the season and the twelve- to fifteen-hour workdays in the off-season. In truth, though, between 6 A.M. and midnight, the phone seldom stops ringing and the beeper seldom stops going off.

A person simply couldn't put in those kinds of hours (which aren't unique to me, of course; they are a major-league baseball executive's lot) without having a deep commitment to the job and a burning passion for it.

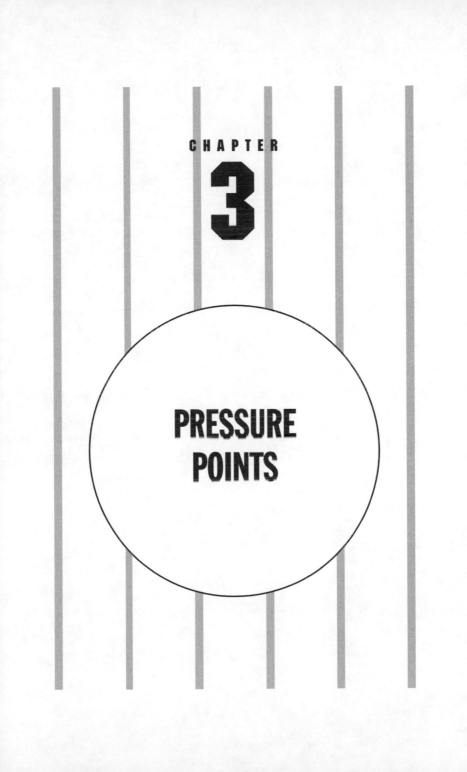

CHAPTER

3

PRESSURE POINTS

I suppose a casual baseball fan, or someone not familiar with the intricacies of a major-league baseball team, might look back at the 1996 season and assume that winning the world championship was easy for the New York Yankees.

We got off to a good start, staked a comfortable lead in our division, held off late-summer challenges from Baltimore and Boston, peaked in the fall play-offs, and then swept the final four games of the World Series against Atlanta. (By the way, that was only the eleventh time in baseball history a world champion has rallied from a two-game deficit, and only the third time a world champion has bounced back to win four straight. It also marked the first time a world champion has swept the final four games after losing the first two at *home*.)

But this is major-league baseball we're talking about. This is New York. And these are the Yankees, the glamour team that back in the 1970s created their own version of the "Bronx Zoo." It's never, ever, a piece of cake in New York.

Pressure points come with the territory.

One of the most critical pressure points in my first

season as Yankees GM had to do with the team's reacquisition of slugging outfielder Darryl Strawberry in midsummer. It was not a decision I endorsed—enthusiastically or otherwise. In fact, at the time the decision was made, I argued against it.

Strawberry, whose once-brilliant career with the New York Mets had unraveled over the years with substance abuse and related personal problems, had been a midseason pickup for the Yankees during the 1995 season. The club had to exercise its option on Strawberry by November 1, 1995, a deadline subsequently extended to the end of the month.

We asked Darryl to go play winter ball in Puerto Rico, to show us he could still play outfield defense at a major-league level. In early November I asked Dick Williams, the well-known former manager who was handling special scouting assignments for the Yankees, to go down to Puerto Rico and monitor Darryl's progress. Dick reported that Strawberry was swinging the bat exceptionally well but that he was DH-ing, that is, appearing in the lineup as a designated hitter. He wasn't getting any work in the outfield.

A couple of weeks later, after getting the point across to Darryl that we were more interested in assessing his defensive skills than his offensive prowess, Gene Michael went to Puerto Rico to make a further evaluation. Stick came back and described Darryl's defense as "iffy" at best.

Near the end of November, after further discussions with Gene and Joe Torre, who had come aboard as Yankees manager earlier that month, I decided not to renew the relationship for 1996. That left Darryl free to make a deal with another team.

By the opening of the 1996 season, Strawberry was still on the street looking for work. To his credit, Darryl didn't give up. He began playing minor-league baseball for the St. Paul Saints, a nonaffiliated team in the independent Class A Northern League, for $2,000 a month.

By all accounts, Strawberry was in good physical condition and taking care of himself. His bat was alive, and he was ripping the caliber of pitching he faced.

In late June, when the Yankees went on a six-game road trip to Cleveland and Minnesota, I accompanied the team. By the time we arrived in Minneapolis, rumors had started swirling that we were interested in obtaining Strawberry's services once again.

I must have fielded two dozen inquiries from the media asking if we were having conversations with Darryl and whether we were trying to lure him back into a Yankees uniform.

"Are you going over to St. Paul to see Strawberry play?" everyone wanted to know.

"No way," I insisted. "If we signed him, where would we play him? What would he add to the mix?"

The answer, in a word, was power. Baseballs had been flying out of ballparks at a record pace. The 1996 season had already been dubbed the "Year of the Homer." Guys like Baltimore's Brady Anderson, Cleveland's Albert Belle, and Oakland's Mark McGwire, among others, were putting up incredible power numbers. Sports talk shows were devoting endless hours to a debate on whether the baseball was juiced.

Let me say here that perhaps the seams on baseballs may have been tightened a bit last season, but the rash of homers in 1996 could be attributed to a variety of reasons. Umpires were calling a constricted strike zone, giving hitters a lot of favorable (1-0, 2-0, 3-1) counts. With expansion and the dilution of talent, hitters were seeing pitches from some triple-A-class pitchers or, in a few isolated cases, double-A-type arms.

Hitters themselves, larger and stronger than in previous eras, were profiting from year-round weight training regimens and innovations like video machines, which allowed them to study pitchers as never before. Finally, balls were flying out of user-friendly parks for power hitters, like Coors Field in Colorado, Camden Yards in Baltimore, and Jacobs Field in Cleveland, to name a few. Throughout the major leagues, dimensions of ballparks have been changed in recent years to feature more offense. Some of the Death Valleys and Yosemite Parks I recall from my playing days, like Forbes Field in Pittsburgh, are long gone.

Given the power surge in the major leagues, George Steinbrenner decided it was time for the New York Yankees to start living up to their nickname—the Bronx Bombers—by participating in the home-run derby.

Our "get 'em on, move 'em along, get 'em in" style was winning ball games (we had opened up a four-game lead in the American League East), but the long ball was conspicuously absent from our attack. Tino Martinez had gotten off to a slow start, and Ruben Sierra's bat was quiet. Out of fourteen teams in the American League, we ranked something like twelfth in home runs.

So, despite recommendations from his GM and field manager that we pass on Strawberry, George exercised his owner's prerogative and rehired him. Following Steinbrenner's orders, I signed Strawberry to a one-year contract with a team option for a second year, and the Yankees agreed to pay some of Darryl's outstanding alimony and child support payments. We brought Strawberry back with the intention of rotating him between outfield and designated hitter.

The deal was announced on July 4, 1996, a pretty good day for fireworks. It also happened to be George Steinbrenner's sixty-sixth birthday, and some people described the return of Darryl Strawberry as George's birthday present to himself.

The New York and national baseball media had a field day with George's unilateral decision making concerning Darryl, although it wasn't without precedent. George Steinbrenner is a hands-on, take-charge type of owner who is totally in control at all times. He makes it perfectly clear who's the boss. He's had success this way, as everyone knows.

Okay, so you're overruled as a GM. What are your options? Pitch a fit? Take your bat and ball and go home? No, you show some flexibility. You adapt. You get over it and move ahead.

I had put forward to George some solid arguments as to why I didn't like the Strawberry transaction. I believed the ball club at that time had other, more critical needs to address. But rather than get bent out of shape by George's decision, I backed it. I chose to keep my focus on the job of building a better team in New York.

We made sure Darryl understood he'd have to work hard and toe the line. We told him we expected him to be a good citizen and a positive force in the dugout. We also had Jose Cardenal, our outfield coach, put in extra hours with Darryl to improve his defense, which has never been the strength of his portfolio.

We welcomed Darryl back into the clubhouse, and, it

should be stressed, he provided a big boost to the ball club with some immediate power. In fact, right after the All-Star break, Strawberry was instrumental in our sweeping a four-game series with Baltimore at Camden Yards. He hit some big home runs, swiped several bases, and got a handful of other key hits during the series.

Coupled with the two games we had tacked on to our lead right before the All-Star break, the four games we picked up in Baltimore extended the Yankees' lead over the Orioles to ten games by mid-July. That gave us a bit of breathing room in what everyone figured to be a close race.

George was basking in the glow of Darryl's big bat. In a game on August 6 at Yankee Stadium against Chicago, Strawberry put on another show, jacking three homers off White Sox pitching. Darryl would finish with 11 dingers in 262 at bats in what was roughly a half season of work.

Let me be the first to say that Darryl was an asset to the team in every way imaginable. He was a good guy in the clubhouse, and he didn't sulk when he sat on the bench. He was a positive role model for our younger players.

I'll admit that when I argued against adding Strawberry to the Yankees roster, I had no idea what a great person Darryl has become. I was wrong about him and

George was right: We needed Darryl to win a championship.

Strawberry's wasn't the only big bat we added to the lineup during the summer. As the July 31 trading deadline loomed, I got together with Randy Smith, the general manager of Detroit, and engineered a trade for Cecil Fielder, the Tigers slugging first baseman.

I should mention that I've known Randy since he was a pup. He's the son of Tal Smith, the president of the Houston Astros and one of my mentors in baseball administration. Prior to the 1995 season, when I was GM of the Astros and Randy had the same job at San Diego, we had orchestrated a twelve-player deal, one of the biggest baseball has seen for decades.

As early as spring training, I had carefully studied the Yankees lineup—on paper and on the field—and concluded that we had a shortage of power from the right side. I immediately thought of big Cecil Fielder as someone who could fill that void. I called Randy Smith to sound him out on a possible deal.

"No way, Bob; we're not trading him," Randy responded. "He's our only marquee name. He's the one guy we have who sells tickets."

"Well, I want you to know I'd like to have him in New York," I said.

The idea of trading for Cecil was put on hold, but it

never went away. Early in the season, accompanying the team on a road trip that went through Detroit, I again broached the subject with Randy. The Tigers had gotten off to a horrible start and were buried deep in the cellar of the American League East. I also knew that we had an excess of what Detroit needed most: pitching.

Randy wasn't budging. He still refused to discuss a trade involving Fielder, but he did tell me to keep in touch with him as the July 31 waiver deadline neared.

"I'll do that," I said. "Just please promise that you won't make any move with Cecil without getting back to me first."

As events unfolded, the Tigers showed little improvement during the early summer. They seemed stuck in a rut. Near the end of July, as the waiver deadline neared, Randy called and asked if I still had an interest in Cecil.

In a word—definitely. We began talking back and forth about a possible deal, tossing out various names and scenarios. Randy and I finally settled on a package that would give Detroit one of our top pitching prospects, Matt Drews, the Yankees' number one pick in the 1993 draft, along with outfielder Ruben Sierra, who was struggling at the plate and being ridden hard by fans at Yankee Stadium. Sierra had pretty much worn out his welcome in New York, and as a GM (and former player), I hate to see that happen.

To sweeten the deal, we were prepared to offer Detroit an undisclosed amount of cash. It was undisclosed but substantial—in the low seven figures.

I knew the kind of quality we were adding to the roster. Cecil's one of the best offensive players in baseball. He'll get the clutch hit and he's a machine at driving home runs. He's led the American League in homers twice and RBI three times. If I'm not mistaken, he has more runs batted in than any major leaguer during the '90s.

The numbers Fielder put up in Detroit and New York for the entire 1996 season—39 homers with 117 RBI—are indicative of his productivity. He's the kind of guy who changes the lights on the outfield scoreboard.

What most people don't know about Cecil, though, is that he's also a great team leader. Fielder is a positive, happy-go-lucky guy whom people naturally like to be around.

Randy and I had reached an agreement in principle; now we needed the boss to sign off. I tracked down George Steinbrenner at the Olympic Village in Atlanta, where he was serving as one of the officials for the United States Olympic Committee during the 1996 Games, and told him what was in the works.

George instructed me to seek permission from Detroit to contact Cecil's agent and see if some compensation could be deferred. I spoke with Fielder's agent, Bob Gilhooly, who said Cecil would be willing to go along. Being the champion that he is, Cecil desperately wanted a shot at winning a World Series ring.

Though our payroll was already over budget, I was able to make the numbers work by using some creative financing with Cecil, deferring some salary and interest payments until 2000 and 2001.

Our decision to acquire Fielder paid consistent dividends, but none bigger than in Game Five of the World Series when Cecil doubled home Charlie Hayes for the only run in the brilliant 1-0 pitchers' duel between Andy Pettitte and John Smoltz.

While George Steinbrenner was all smiles about the Fielder deal, he began fuming about another trade I made on the very same day: an exchange of right-handed relief pitchers with Florida. Based on recommendations from Joe Torre and pitching coach Mel Stottlemyre, I sent Mark Hutton to the Marlins for David Weathers.

Hutton, who had been one of Steinbrenner's favorites but whose career had been plagued by injury, including a serious groin tear, got off to a great start in Florida, winning several consecutive games as a starter and posting a good ERA.

Meanwhile, Weathers came to New York and started getting lit up like the Christmas tree at Rockefeller

Center. After four or five rocky outings, Steinbrenner had seen enough.

"You've been duped," he bellowed, using one of his favorite words. "I want Weathers sent down to Columbus. Get him out of here."

I tried to stand my ground, to no avail. George insisted that we send Weathers down. So, reluctantly, I shipped Weathers out to Columbus, praying he would regain some confidence.

Fortunately, Weathers did. The time David spent in the minor leagues helped him collect his thoughts and clear the playing field, so to speak. He refocused on a fresh start.

We brought David back in September and added him to our postseason roster. That decision turned out to be particularly astute, because Weathers pitched superbly throughout the play-offs, posting a 2-0 record and getting us out of some sticky situations against Texas and Baltimore.

Weathers's rocky beginning, though, was still fresh on Steinbrenner's mind when we reached mid-August. That's when George asked me what the one thing was the Yankees needed to get over the hump and advance deep into the postseason. "A quality left-handed reliever," I replied.

When George asked who might be available, I told him we had an eye on Graeme (pronounced Grame)

Lloyd, a tall (6-foot-7) and rangy southpaw, who's a native of Australia and who was having a creditable season with the Milwaukee Brewers. Our scouts were high on Lloyd, thinking he could get us through some special situations and matchups.

I called Sal Bando, the Brewers' GM, and started talking about a deal for Lloyd. We finally agreed in principle to a package: The Yankees would send Bob Wickman, a right-handed relief pitcher, and Gerald Williams, our fourth outfielder, to Milwaukee for Lloyd and Pat Listach, an outfielder and utility infielder.

What appeared to be a straightforward transaction turned out to be anything but routine. A day or two before the deal was consummated (August 23), Listach fouled a pitch off his right foot. When he arrived in New York, he was hobbled. He couldn't go.

Sal Bando assured me that X rays taken in Milwaukee on Listach's foot were clean. I ordered a second set of X rays and that they too came back negative. But the pain in Listach's foot persisted, so shortly after Pat arrived in New York, Dr. Hershon, our physician, decided we should do a bone scan. The procedure revealed a broken bone.

Listach's injury didn't set well with any of us, especially George Steinbrenner. First, he wanted to have the trade rescinded, claiming the Brewers had sent us damaged goods. Then George insisted on receiving additional compensation from Milwaukee. Bando agreed to pay Pat Listach's salary for the remainder of the season.

Complicating matters, though, was the performance of Lloyd. After a good first outing, he started getting shelled. After his third rough outing in a row, Lloyd admitted that he had received a cortisone shot, to treat tendinitis in his ailing arm, ten days prior to the trade. Later, tests showed Graeme had a floating bone chip in his left elbow (which was removed during surgery after the World Series).

Steinbrenner went through the roof when he learned about Lloyd's injury. He told the New York press that I had been duped by Milwaukee·and sold a bill of goods. He initiated legal action against Milwaukee owner Bud Selig, the acting commissioner. (The suit, still pending as I write this, has never come to court; but to make amends and mollify Steinbrenner's anger, the Brewers sent us right-handed pitcher Ricky Bones and later threw in minor-league infielder Gabby Martinez, one of the top prospects in their organization.)

Understandably, George began venting frustration all over the place. He told the New York press that my job was on the line. The headlines in the newspaper read: "Watson Was Duped." There's that word again. *Duped.*

I knew my job was hanging in the balance. For a

period of a week or so, I went to the office wondering if it would be my last day as Yankees GM.

But I didn't overreact to negative media coverage that painted me as a buffoon or the village idiot. I didn't like it, but I knew I could tolerate it. The same media that early in the season had labeled Joe Torre as "Clueless Joe" was now holding him up as a great manager, so I knew how quickly attitudes could change. Besides, I have never tried to seek the media's approval.

I knew in my heart we had performed the necessary diligence. I knew my staff and I had done our homework and asked the right questions. Misled, maybe. Duped? I don't know about that.

After consultation with Dr. Hershon and our trainer, Gene Monahan, we decided to rest Lloyd for several weeks, hoping he would regain his arm strength in time for the play-offs. Which, as events unfolded, he did. Graeme came through in the clutch in each of the play-off series. He made a total of eight appearances, pitching 5.1 innings without allowing a single run. He was the winning pitcher in Game Four of the World Series. He came up big.

And, during the time Graeme was portrayed in the press as a failure, he handled the situation like a true champion; he didn't allow the criticism to deter him from his work.

Looking back, I can say without a moment's

hesitation that the New York Yankees wouldn't be world champions today were it not for the contributions of Graeme Lloyd and David Weathers.

BACK TO
THAT GLORIOUS DAY

So there I was, standing in the Yankees clubhouse after the World Series trophy presentation, watching the ballplayers gleefully spray one another with champagne and hearing George Steinbrenner tell an interviewer, "This team represents all New York, because they don't quit. New Yorkers don't quit. All the problems, we don't quit in this city. This team, more than any I've seen, exemplifies that spirit."

Instead of being able to revel in the moment and soak up the excitement of such a boisterous and joyous atmosphere, I was being hounded with questions from the media about the recent controversy with our pitching staff.

"Guys, come on, give me a break," I said. "Let's talk about what happened on the field, not off of it. The New York Yankees have just won the world championship. Give me some time to enjoy the moment, okay?"

The media later wrote that I had been "vindicated" by Lloyd's performance in the postseason. I'm not sure whether vindication is the correct word for what went down in September and October, but I am convinced my staff and I had gone about our business properly.

We trusted our judgment. We had faith in our own ability to evaluate talent and set up the roster. I stood behind everyone on the staff 100 percent, as a general manager should.

Does that mean I think we're incapable of making mistakes? Of course not. We are human beings. We have imperfections. We don't have crystal balls that allow us to see into the future. Consequently, we all make our share of bad choices and misjudgments.

All you can do in the face of extreme pressure is go about your business in a professional manner. Be prepared—by that I mean do all the necessary homework and background—and then take your best shot.

I've also learned in life that if you expect good results, you can achieve them. You will find that good things happen when you believe in yourself.

As for having had my job on the line, as for having been set up as a scapegoat if things had turned out differently in the 1996 play-offs—that's the nature of this job. General managers, like field managers, are always under the heat when the objective is to win ball games and the results don't go our way.

Our business is a meritocracy. Win, and you're able to enjoy the spoils of victory. Lose, and someone else will be summoned to take your place. Job security, such as it is, depends on performance—something everybody can see every day in the win-loss column.

The way the system works, only the strongest survive. Well, guess what? Bob Watson survived.

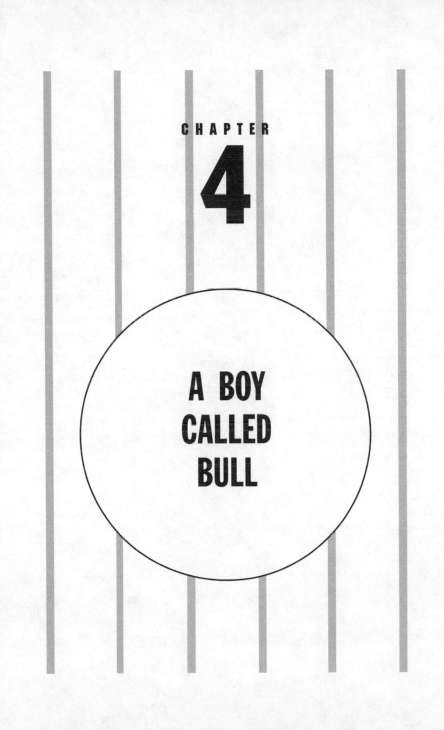

CHAPTER

4

A BOY CALLED BULL

I was born on April 10, 1946, in what was then called the east side of Los Angeles but now is known, somewhat notoriously, as South Central L.A. It's the part of the city where all those sociological movies like *Boyz N the Hood* are based.

The violence and squalor vividly portrayed in those movies were absent from my youth. In the late 1940s and 1950s, our neighborhood was alive with the happy sounds of kids playing in the street or over in the park. Kids having fun.

Among those children were my brother, Arthur, and me. As youngsters, we played our own version of baseball, using a broomstick as a bat and wads of duct tape or electrical tape as a ball. Arthur pretended to be the New York Yankees, and I was the Milwaukee Braves or Washington Senators. We set up our own field and rules.

Later, as our mastery with the broomstick bat increased, we took our game to a new level by using bottle caps as the ball. If you could make good contact with a bottle cap, which darted, dipped, and swerved, you were doing something. I've always believed the hand-eye coordination skills I developed learning to hit bottle caps helped me become a major leaguer.

My parents, Wilma and Eddie Watson, by all accounts had a rocky relationship. Their marriage lasted just long enough to produce two boys, Robert Jose (the middle name came courtesy of my dad's best friend) and Arthur.

When my parents broke up in 1947, they gave me to my grandparents, the Stewarts, and gave Arthur to the Stewarts' best friends and next-door neighbors, Henry and Ruby Sandoz. The Sandozes owned the courts where both families lived. From birth, my brother received the name Arthur Sandoz. Though we had different last names, we were as close as any brothers could be.

My mother later remarried and gave birth to three other children—my half brother, Lawrence Perkins, and my half sisters, Francis and Brenda Perkins.

◆

MY FIRST "AT BAT"

My career in baseball began one day in the spring of 1954, when my grandmother and I went to pay a visit to her sister, Velma Mitchell, who lived in the Avalon projects in east Los Angeles, directly across the street from Green Meadows playground.

While the ladies visited on the stoop, my attention shifted to a group of boys playing baseball over at the playground. I stood transfixed for several minutes, then asked Grandmother for permission to go over to the playground to watch. When I got there, I realized the kids were trying out for some kind of summer league and that registration of players was taking place.

I raced back across the street and asked Grandmother if I could sign up. She said yes, so I wrote my name on the list. I put down Aunt Velma's address as my residence, in case living outside the Green Meadows neighborhood would make me ineligible.

I borrowed someone's glove, went out in the field to throw and catch, and wound up being assigned to one of the teams. Robert Jose Watson, all of eight years old, was about to be ushered into organized baseball.

My first at bat in official competition was prophetic: As the pitcher wound up and fired, the ball came floating up toward the plate looking as big as a beach ball. It wasn't so much a question of whether I could hit it but rather which part of the ball I wanted to attack.

I took as mighty a swing as an eight-year-old can muster. At impact, the ball shot off of my bat and flew far beyond the left fielder. The bat's crack against the rawhide sounded like a pistol shot. The sensation was immense and powerful, and, watching as the ball sailed away, I said to myself, *Wow!* I skipped around the bases, scarcely containing my joy.

I played the first half of the game at third base, then

shifted to catcher for the final few innings. I had no trouble adapting to the new position, one many kids shy away from. I wasn't scared of the batter standing beside me, twirling the pine. I didn't flinch or blink when the batter swung. I had a strong enough arm to peg the ball back to the pitcher or all the way to second base.

From the moment I put on the gear (the "tools of ignorance") and squatted behind the plate, I started thinking that being the catcher was the most important job on the field. You were at the center of the baseball universe, having a hand in every play.

No doubt countless thousands of little boys in America who hit home runs in their first Little League at bat, or first official game, go to bed that same night dreaming of becoming the next Mickey Mantle or Willie Mays or Ken Griffey Jr. or Barry Bonds. On a spring night in 1954 in east Los Angeles, with the wind blowing in off the Pacific Ocean, I dreamed of becoming the next Roy Campanella or Yogi Berra—a power-hitting, big-league catcher.

Roughly 99.999999 percent of those little home-run hitters get sidetracked by other sports such as football or basketball, or by cars or girls or goodness knows what. Either that, or they find they can't catch up with a live fastball or hit the curve.

But my focus never wandered away from baseball, and my bat never slowed down. I embraced the gift.

It was as though I somehow knew, from that very first swing in that first game, that I had a date with destiny. The funny thing was that even as I tossed around in bed and tugged at the sheets that night, too keyed up by the sensation of bat meeting ball to sleep, I could sense the awakening of a strange and wonderful force within me.

A LARGE ADVANTAGE

I was always large for my age, with a big frame and big bones. I suppose I got that from my father, who is around 6′1″ or 6′2″ and probably 210 pounds. By the time I was ten and playing in three separate youth leagues on Saturdays, slipping in and out of different uniforms in the backseat of my grandparents' 1937 Plymouth, I looked like a teenager. By the time I reached my teens and was jacking baseballs over the fence, up on the rooftop, and out into the street, I was 6 feet tall and 195 pounds. I looked like an adult.

My imposing size, however, didn't stop some thugs from jumping me a few days after my grandparents and I moved into a new house near the Green Meadows playground when I was fifteen. I'd gone over to the park looking for a pickup game of baseball, when out of the blue came four guys, wielding sticks and a motorcycle chain. I guess they were the neighborhood's self-appointed welcoming committee. Some welcome.

I was thoroughly slugged, stomped, kicked, bitten, and beaten. My back, ribs, kidneys, and legs were bruised. My head felt like pavement on the working side of a jackhammer. As I was being beaten, I studied the face of one of my tormentors, trying to take my mind off the battering.

I limped home from the playground, looking as beat up as Clint Eastwood in one of his spaghetti westerns, and collapsed on the couch in our living room. While my grandmother went to get some ice for my bruises and bandages for my bleeding, my grandfather surveyed the damage and said, "Son, you have to go back over to the park and stand your ground. Otherwise, you won't be able to live in this neighborhood."

So the next day, aching all over, I went back to the park and tracked down the guy whose mug I had memorized in such detail. Without a stick, chain, or the backing of his trio of buddies, he didn't seem so tough. I grabbed him, wrestled him down, and started giving him a taste of the licking he'd helped dish out.

For the next week, I found that guy after school every day and gave him another whipping. For whatever reason, his buddies didn't show up to defend him. I never ran into any of those other three guys again.

After that one incident, I had the neighborhood's

respect. Grandfather had been right, as usual; I had to stand my ground or become a whipping boy. Looking back now, as a professed man of Christ, I can't condone the violence and would probably try to negotiate my way out of fighting with those guys.

On the other hand, I've learned that in life you have to stand up for yourself or you'll get walked on, especially in the ghetto.

It's funny, some people think Christians are supposed to be pacifists. They misinterpret Jesus' life and reach the conclusion he was a passive man. In truth, he was a big, rugged carpenter. He threw over the tables in the temple and tossed out the moneylenders. He showed aggressiveness, even anger, when those emotions were justified. He could have batted cleanup.

I never had any more trouble after I refused to back down from intimidation. I went back to playing baseball and hitting home runs. The supervisor of Green Meadows playground, Mr. Regenboggen, offered me a job. Suddenly I found myself getting paid to hang out at the park and play baseball, something I gladly would have done for nothing. I was in teenage heaven.

THE BULL

My size came into play again later in high school when the baseball coach at Fremont High, Phil Pote, started handing out nicknames to the guys on our team. He asked me who my favorite ballplayers were, and I told him Tommy Davis and John Roseboro of the Los Angeles Dodgers and Orlando Cepeda of the San Francisco Giants.

"They call Cepeda the Baby Bull," I said, repeating something I'd heard Vin Scully, the Dodgers' play-by-play man, say during a broadcast.

"Well, you're too big to be a baby anything," Coach Pote pointed out. "So we'll just call you 'Bull.'"

The nickname stuck. One day soon after, I was goofing around with one of my teammates and best friends, Dwight Kenney. We were sparring with each other, exchanging jabs on the arm. Dwight was acting like Cassius Clay, bobbing and weaving and throwing light punches from different angles. He gave me a feint, and the next thing I knew he'd popped me squarely between the eyes.

The jab wasn't all that hard and wasn't meant to be malicious or anything, but I was momentarily blinded. As I groped about, I banged into a small seedling of a tree, which became uprooted. It fell right at my feet.

All the guys marveled at the sight of me, dazed and

bleary, standing next to a flattened tree. "Man," said Dwight, "only a bull could uproot a tree like that."

That's how, at age sixteen, I became Bob "Bull" Watson. To this day, many of my closest friends still call me Bull. It's a handle I like. To me, the nickname Bull suggests strength, power, optimism, and perseverance. When people say they are "bullish" about something, they are talking in a positive manner. There's also a bit of foreboding in the name: Don't mess with the Bull or you may get the horns.

ON THE DIAMOND

My years at Fremont High produced more highlights on the baseball diamond than in the classroom. I wasn't what you'd call a scholar, though I paid attention in class, did the required homework assignments, and was never a disruptive presence. I had a pretty good head for numbers and was handy with a slide rule. But writing essays never was my forte.

My best subject in high school was technical drawing. Looking back, had I not pursued a career in professional baseball, I likely would have become a technical illustrator. When I attended junior college for a year, I took classes in mechanical drafting and airbrushing. I knew I needed to develop a craft in case my aspirations in base-ball didn't pan out.

But the real education I received as a teenager came on the baseball diamond, where I made second team all-city catcher in my senior year. At Fremont High I played with some great athletes, many of whom would go on to make a name for themselves in the major leagues.

Readers may recognize names like Bobby Tolan, Paul Blair, Roy White, Estes Banks (who wound up playing pro football), Dwight Kenney, Leon McFadden, Gary Boyd, Roscoe Proctor, Dennis Gilbert (now a well-known sports agent), Bobby Watkins, Reggie Smith, Willie Craw-ford, Brock Davis, Paul Jefferson, Carl Moore, Ross Sapp, and Charlie Murray (Eddie Murray's older brother).

On our South Park summer team, sponsored by the Pittsburgh Pirates, we had Tolan, Blair, Smith, White, Dock Ellis, Don Wilson, Enos Cabell, George Hendrick, Chet Lemon, Wayne Simpson, and Dan Ford.

Why, you may wonder, did so many great baseball players come out of Los Angeles? Let me paint the pic-ture for you:

We enjoyed beautiful weather year-round in south-ern California. The sky was blue and clear and the infamous L.A. smog was no big deal. Given those cham-ber-of-commerce-type conditions, kids wanted to be out-doors getting exercise, playing ball.

The relocation of the Dodgers franchise from Brooklyn to Los Angeles for the 1958 season had created a groundswell of excitement about pro baseball in the city. The heroics of Jackie Robinson, who broke baseball's racial barrier in 1947 (with the Dodgers, it should be noted), and all the other great African-American players who followed him, stoked the fires of ambition among young black athletes like me. We had something to aim at, and we weren't shut out of the process.

Los Angeles was a big baseball town in the '50s and '60s. In addition to the Dodgers, the Cubs had an AAA Pacific Coast League team that played at Wrigley Field, a replica of the famous stadium in Chicago. The Hollywood Stars had a large following, and in 1961 the American League set up an expansion franchise, the California Angels. Meanwhile, the Los Angeles Lakers, even with Elgin Baylor and Jerry West, hadn't caught on as the hottest sports ticket in town. That honor was reserved for baseball.

In addition, when I was growing up, the television set had yet to put a stranglehold on so many young lives. Kids were less likely to be indoor couch potatoes. The "Malling of America" was still two decades away. Electronic games like Atari and Nintendo were still ideas percolating in someone's imagination.

Kids still played outside—and with each other. Even gang members in the neighborhood, tough guys living on the fringe, would stop by the park and play pickup baseball games.

The city's streets weren't so mean then. My friends and I played baseball in the park, day and night, year-round. We honed our skills through the sheer repetition of doing something we loved virtually 365 days a year. We were the equivalent of young boys and girls who, after years of spending their days at the local golf course, play-ing thirty-six holes a day, hitting buckets of practice balls, and practicing chipping, pitching, and putting, wind up on the PGA Tour.

I know that some people, especially those in the Northeast, refer to basketball as the "city game," but in Los Angeles, when I was coming up, the primary game kids played was baseball. And many guys I knew from the neighborhood played it exceptionally well.

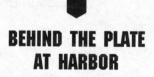

BEHIND THE PLATE
AT HARBOR

After high school, I attended Harbor Junior College in Wilmington, California, during the fall of '63 and spring of '64. I took classes in mechanical drafting and some core requirements and, as a walk-on, joined the baseball team. I won the job as starting catcher and hit .371, making the all-conference team.

My play behind the plate at Harbor JC caught the eye of a West Coast scout for the Houston Astros, Karl Kuehl. He told me that I had the potential to be a professional ballplayer and encouraged me to sign a free-agent contract.

There was never any doubt I would. Some of my friends from Fremont High, guys like Bobby Tolan, Willie Crawford, Paul Blair, and Dwight Kenney, had already signed contracts and were playing in the minor leagues. I was ready to take the big step myself.

I wasn't a bonus baby by any means. Houston gave me the grand sum of $2,000 plus a round-trip plane ticket to Florida (the return portion was in case things didn't work out). In February 1965, two months short of my nineteenth birthday, I said good-bye to family and friends, boarded a TWA jet at LAX and flew to Melbourne, Florida, where I caught a bus to take me to the Astros' camp in Cocoa.

I had no idea where the road might lead—certainly not to Yankee Stadium and a World Series championship thirty-one years later. All I knew for sure as I left California was that I was heading out on an adventure many teenage boys dream about but few actually experience. And that, with belief in myself and a little help from the Man upstairs, I could get the job done as a professional ballplayer.

Little did I know, however, just how many obstacles awaited.

CHAPTER

5

OVERCOMING
THE
ODDS

One of my fondest memories in baseball is of that first training camp with the Houston Astros in 1965. I can use a word like *fond* now, three decades removed from the actual events, but at the time I would have chosen another word to describe the experience. Perhaps *wacky* or *crazy*.

The Astros were spending their first spring in Cocoa, where they had built a training complex with several diamonds on top of a swamp. To make way for base paths and batting cages, the grounds crew had applied truckloads of topsoil to the swamp, disturbing the native inhabitants, a sizable and varied collection of snakes, scorpions, and vermin.

The players were housed in a dormitory, which was quickly labeled the "Astro Hilton," given the lack of amenities (like hot water). Evidently, Astros owner Judge Roy F. Hofheinz had put so much money into the Astrodome—which opened in time for the 1965 season and which, as the first domed stadium in baseball, was billed as the "Eighth Wonder of the World"—that he had little left over to spend on necessities in Cocoa: decent lodging for the players, for example. The saving grace of the whole experience was the food Morrison's Cafeteria provided. At mealtime, we really chowed down.

Upon waking each morning, we shook out our shoes, as instructed, just in case scorpions or tarantulas had invaded them during the night. The prospect alone could cost a person several hours' worth of decent sleep. So could the humming of mosquitoes, which congregated around our quarters and seemed to be as large as horseflies.

Each day before the players took the field in Cocoa, the groundskeeper would take a shotgun with him and patrol the field. On an average day, he probably killed a half-dozen copperheads and water moccasins, and the occasional rattlesnake, before practice even began.

If you were playing the outfield, standing well away from the heavy traffic, it was hard to concentrate on what was happening at the plate. That's because your eyes had a tendency to dart around, looking to see if goodness-knows-what might be slithering toward you. I can still recall the hilarious sight of outfielders making a mad dash for the infield during the middle of an inning. I say hilarious because that never happened to me.

Not that I was a long shot to make the squad or anything, but the Astros assigned me uniform number 202. That alone should have had me sharpening up pencils for drafting class.

I felt like a bull at a cattle auction: little more than a

piece of meat. But, overall, I did a pretty decent job of impressing the Houston coaches. They liked my short, compact stroke and the fact that I hit the ball hard up the middle.

My first at bat in Cocoa—shades of the Green Meadows playground eleven years earlier—was a home run, a towering blast out to right center. As much as I would like to have retrieved the ball for a keepsake, I never once entertained the notion of going out to look for it after the workout ended. I'd seen enough swamp creatures, thank you. The ball could sleep with the snakes.

The pitch, incidentally, had been a curveball, down and away. As happens at every level in baseball, the guys who can handle the hook quickly separate themselves from those who can't. I mean, it's a common occurrence at baseball camps to see some hopeful calling his wife or parents to say, "I'm coming home. I can't hit the curveball."

Fortunately, I was able to call my grandparents back in Los Angeles and say, "Looks like I'll be sticking around for a while. I can hit the curve."

As events unfolded, I stayed throughout spring training, and when the Astros broke camp in late March, I was assigned to Houston's Class A affiliate in Salisbury, North Carolina.

Now came one of the hardest obstacles that I, like the other minority ballplayers of that era, had to endure in

baseball: racial ostracism. I quickly discovered upon ar-
riving in Salisbury, a town of perhaps 15,000 located half-
way between Charlotte and Winston-Salem, that as a
black man I could not stay in the hotel that housed my
teammates. Nor could I eat at the hotel cafe with them.
"Sorry, Son," I was told. "That's just the way things are
done around here."

I was shocked. I couldn't believe what was happening, or that people didn't seem to care. Sure, I had heard
and read about racial injustice in the South, but this was
1965. The Civil War had been over for *one hundred* years.
The Civil Rights movement and freedom marches led by
Dr. Martin Luther King Jr. had been going on for several
years, and the "Great Society" legislative agenda being
championed by President Lyndon B. Johnson was moving forward.

I had never experienced this kind of overt racism
growing up in Los Angeles. There, the barriers you encountered were economic, not racial. The city was open
for blacks: We could go anywhere and do anything, if we
had the money. We were never rejected or denied admis-
sion because of the color of our skin. In Salisbury,
though, doors were slammed shut in my face.

Finally, providence appeared in the person of a Mr.
Gaither, a diminutive black man in his sixties or seventies
who let me board at his house and charged me eight
dollars a week. I could never thank him enough.

Racism showed itself in other ways. For example, a local restaurant sponsored a promotion with the club whereby any time a Salisbury player hit a home run, he earned a free steak dinner. A Salisbury steak, as it were.

Because I was black, however, I was never allowed to collect my prize. The people at the restaurant wouldn't even let me take a steak out the back door and eat it in my room at Mr. Gaither's place. So I wound up giving my gift certificates to my teammates. Some "gift."

Being only nineteen years old and feeling like a stranger in a strange land, I pretty much kept to myself in Salisbury. For entertainment away from the ballpark, I bought a portable record player and wore out the grooves on the five albums I purchased—James Brown, the Four Tops, the Supremes, the Temptations, and Smokey Robinson and the Miracles. I de-waxed those discs.

Trust me, I would be hard to beat on *Jeopardy* if the category were black musicians of the late 1960s. ("Give me Motown for $500, Alex.")

To economize (I was trying to send as much of my $400-a-month paycheck back home to my grandparents as possible) I restricted my diet. I ate Wheaties twice a day, morning and night, hoping that the Breakfast of Champions would prove to be the Dinner of Champions as well. When I wanted to have a gourmet meal, I ate a bologna and cheese sandwich.

I spent most of my time alone in the evenings reading and rereading the three books in my possession: Ted Williams's book on the art of hitting, the Houston Astros team manual (which I could recite from memory), and a copy of the New Testament and the Psalms, which Phil Pote had given me.

I read a lot from Psalms and memorized a few favorite verses, like John 3:16 ("For God so loved the world that He gave His only begotten Son, that whoever believes in Him should not perish but have everlasting life") and John 3:3 ("Jesus answered and said to him, 'Most assuredly, I say to you, unless one is born again, he cannot see the kingdom of God' ").

I let my bat do most of my talking. In yet another case of déjà vu, I hit a home run in my first at bat with Salisbury. During the season I demonstrated potential to move up in the minor-league system. My offensive production that season was such that on the days I didn't catch, which were few and far between, management wanted my bat in the lineup and put me out in left field.

There I encountered a subtle, but insidious, form of racism. The ballpark at Salisbury had no warning track, meaning that on deep shots to the outfield you were at the mercy of the other outfielders to warn you of how close you were to the fence.

On August 6, 1965, I was playing left field when a batter hit a shot to the power alley. I could see that if the ball stayed in the park it would be my play, so I raced back as hard as I could. In my haste, I overlooked the fact that the center fielder for Salisbury was one of the biggest racists on the team. His frequent use of racial slurs gave him away.

His shout to warn me of danger never came. Running at full speed, I crashed headlong into the outfield wall. The impact was so forceful—they don't call me Bull because I'm a delicate creature—that I broke my left wrist and right shoulder. Those two injuries, sustained in my very first season of pro ball, would bother me for years to come. I had to learn to play with pain.

I blacked out momentarily from the collision with the unyielding wall. When I came to, I witnessed one of the strangest sights I've ever seen in baseball: Our right fielder, Ed Moxey, who was from the Bahamas and black like me, had raced over and begun punching out the center fielder.

Meanwhile, the runner was circling the bases for an inside-the-park homer. But Ed didn't care. He was busy thumping the center fielder and, much to my delight, thumping him good. I wouldn't have minded doing the job myself, but I was in no condition to take my revenge.

The next day, my left wrist in a cast and my right shoulder in a sling, I was flown to Houston for medical evaluation. It didn't take a genius from Johns Hopkins or the Mayo Clinic to see I'd be on the shelf for several months to come.

That evening in Houston, when I returned to my hotel room, I clicked on the television and saw live news reports from the Watts section of Los Angeles, not far from my old neighborhood, where riots had begun. I watched in silence and blinked in amazement when I recognized, right there on the TV screen, the Green Meadows playground of my youth. My old park was a staging area already filled with armored tanks.

I had immediate concern for the safety of my family. My grandfather worked part-time at a corner store, and I could see on TV that storefronts on that same street had been torched and were aflame. I was sick with worry and fear. Fortunately, everyone in my family was all right, but I didn't learn that right away, because phone service into that area was disrupted for several weeks.

After my experiences that summer in Salisbury, feeling shunned and not fully part of society, I could relate to some of the rage residents in Watts were expressing in such a forceful, demonstrative manner. Their anger reflected the deep schisms in society.

ANOTHER KIND
OF TRAINING CAMP

During the fall of '65, while my injuries healed, I joined the U.S. Marine Corps reserves and went to boot camp in San Diego. Many ballplayers, including household names like Rod Carew, Joe Rudi, Rick Monday (as I recall, the first ballplayer called up by the draft board for the Vietnam War), and a lifelong friend of mine, Steve Free, who played with the Minnesota Twins, did the same.

With my injured right shoulder, I was unable to fire a rifle. Even after corrective surgery, my shoulder couldn't take the pounding of an M-14; so I became, I suppose, one of the few Marines who ever qualified for rifleman training by shooting a .45 pistol.

I learned some important life lessons during my military experience. I valued the discipline, especially the physical conditioning and chain of command. I appreciated all the preparation and attention to detail. Show me someone who's been through Marine Corps training, and I'll show you someone trained to get the job done right, with no shortcuts or excuses.

Given the gravity of the situation—most of my fellow trainees were headed to the battlefield in Southeast Asia, a bleak prospect that caused two guys in the company to commit suicide during basic training—I grew up in the space of a few months.

I was named platoon leader and then platoon guide, the guy who gets to carry the banner in parades before staff. I made PFC out of boot camp then went to Camp Pendleton for infantry training and made lance corporal. The promotions were meaningful because I was a reservist, not on "regular" duty. I was proud that I made sergeant after only three years of reserve duty, something that generally requires four to six years to achieve. I served with a chopper squadron at, of all places, the *El Toro* naval base in San Diego. Not a bad place for a Bull.

After that close encounter with an outfield wall in Salisbury, injuries continued to impede my career for the next several years. Nevertheless, I marched resolutely up the Astros organization toward the major leagues. At the end of the 1966 season, after hitting .302 and making the all-star team in the Florida State League, I underwent shoulder surgery at Centinela Hospital in Los Angeles (performed by Dr. Robert Kerlan, the Dodgers team physician) and had three pins inserted in my right shoulder.

Dan Blocker, who played Hoss on *Bonanza*—one of my favorite TV shows—happened to be in the next room at the hospital. After I introduced myself, he told me he'd try to keep up with my career. He seemed like a genuinely nice man.

Before the operation, I had made my major-league debut in Los Angeles, albeit a cameo appearance. I came to bat late in a game against veteran left-hander Claude Osteen. One of my heroes, John Roseboro, was catching for the Dodgers, and he asked me what pitch I wanted to see.

I told him I didn't care. "Throw me anything," I said.

"Well, here comes a slider," Roseboro said, and I promptly hit a wicked one-hopper down the third base line that, in the Florida State League, would have headed to the corner for an easy double.

This, however, was Dodger Stadium. The big time. Veteran Junior Gilliam made a dive to his right and backhanded the ball cleanly. From his knees, he threw me out at first base.

"Welcome to the major leagues, Kid," said Ron Fairly, the Dodgers first baseman, as I crossed the bag.

When I got back to the bench my Astro teammates said I'd been the victim of a big-time play. "No, that's not big time." I shook my head. "That's robbery."

The day before, I had been out on deck, ready to pinch-hit against Sandy Koufax, when manager Grady Hatton called me back for Felix Mantilla. I regretted not having the chance to face Koufax, the best pitcher of his generation, who retired after the 1966 season.

In 1967, I remained injury free (not counting lingering soreness in the right shoulder from that collision with the outfield wall) during a season split between Amarillo of the Texas League (AA) and Oklahoma City of the Pacific Coast League (AAA). At the end of the season, I had a brief stint with the Astros, hitting .214 in fourteen at bats. During a weekend series in Pittsburgh I got my first major-league hit, off Pirate veteran Vern Law, and my first major-league home run, a blast off left-hander Jim Shellenback that cleared the fence in left-center field and traveled about 430 feet.

During the off-season, I met the woman who would become the love of my life, Carol Le'fer. Carol lived in a house next door to my good friend Dwight Kenney. On December 2, 1967, she invited us to a birthday party she was hosting the next evening for her cousin, Mark Lee. Carol and I got along so well at the party that the next morning, a Sunday, I showed up at her doorstep again and we went to church.

The following week, we went on a double date, but I was more interested in Carol than the girl I was with, and she seemed more interested in me than the guy she was with.

Carol and I started dating steadily shortly thereafter. We had a number of dates before I had to report for spring training camp in mid-February and, before I knew it, I had fallen head over heels in love.

Carol was full of curiosity and imagination. She had a great sense of fashion, honed by years of flipping through magazines like *Vogue* and *Harper's Bazaar* and studying the details of every dress, gown, ensemble, and shoe she saw in the advertisements. She also had a passion for movies, especially old black-and-white films from the 1930s and 1940s. She loved listening to the dialogue and carefully studying the fashions.

She wasn't exactly a baseball novice. Her mother, Ella, and her aunt, Barbara, had once played on an all-girls baseball team that traveled around southern California. Carol had attended a few Dodgers games with some of her friends and learned how to read a box score.

Right before I left for Florida, we went to see *Bonnie and Clyde* over on the Hollywood Strip. Coming out of the theater, walking hand in hand, we noticed a jewelry store nearby. On the spur of the moment, I proposed marriage and she accepted. We ventured into the store and bought an engagement ring.

◼

YET ANOTHER INJURY

In 1968, I started the season at Oklahoma City and was hitting a torrid .395 when the Astros called me up in

June. Houston manager Harry "the Hat" Walker wanted my bat in the lineup, which was great, but he decided to have me lead off, which wasn't. I must have been one of the largest, and slowest, leadoff men in baseball history. I definitely didn't have a green light to run whenever I wanted.

That same summer, I tore up my ankle in Chicago. The day before the injury I was sitting in a hotel room, talking long-distance to Carol and watching the riots going on during the Democratic National Convention. From my perspective, it looked as if the Chicago police could swing clubs at least as well as the Chicago Cubs, if not the White Sox.

The next day, with a fine mist falling on Wrigley Field, I led off against the Cubs ace, Ferguson Jenkins. I hit a curveball into the corner in left, and when Billy Williams fumbled it for a moment I briefly entertained the idea of trying for three bases.

Instead, I rounded second base and slammed on the brakes. Below the damp topsoil, I discovered, was hard, dry ground on which my cleats caught. With all that forward momentum being stopped so sharply, I rolled my ankle badly and collapsed in a heap.

I crawled back to second base, waved to the umpire for a time-out and looked down to inspect the damage. My ankle had swelled, in an instant, to twice its normal size. It was broken.

I had to wear a cast from ankle to midthigh for sixteen weeks. On October 5, 1968, the day after the cast came off, Carol and I were married.

Two weeks later we left to play winter ball in the Dominican Republic. For Carol, the trip to the Caribbean represented a big adventure: She had never been farther away from Los Angeles than the San Diego Zoo.

Carol tells great stories about our time in the coastal town of San Pedro de Marcois, where we shared a house with Leon and Jackie McFadden, had our own housekeeper, and subsisted on a diet of Campbell's soup, hot dogs, and lime Kool-Aid.

For example, if Carol and Jackie didn't attend our games, which were played at night, they had to sit at home in total darkness. That's because all the electricity in the area was needed to crank up the outfield lights at the ballpark. So they stocked up on candles and bought a transistor radio to listen to the broadcasts. They learned to recognize the words *fa-oool boow-la*.

When Carol and Jackie decided to venture out to one of our games, the team arranged for a driver—perhaps I should say bodyguard—named Nando to provide transportation. Nando didn't speak English. Carol and Jackie didn't speak Spanish. But they didn't need a translator when they saw that next to Nando on the front seat was a large *pistola*. Carol took one look at that big gun and said to Jackie, "Do you think ballgames down here will be fun?"

Carol claims that two lifetimes flashed before her eyes while Nando negotiated the dark dirt roads before he delivered them safely to the ballpark. She still talks about the vibrant atmosphere at the game, especially all the people milling outside the stadium, eating food cooked in what looked like large kettledrums, and the male dancers, dressed in brightly colored satin clothes doing dance steps on the top of our dugout to the driving rhythm of drums.

It was a short trip, however. I reinjured my ankle running the bases, and Carol contracted a parasite that required her immediate hospitalization when we got back home. She was seriously ill for several weeks.

The ankle would never completely heal, though the running part of baseball was never my meal ticket. I could still swing the bat, bad ankle or not. But I still wasn't free from racism.

◆

OTHER BOUTS WITH RACISM

Unfortunately, racial ostracism remained part of the equation as I battled through injury after injury. When the Astros assigned me to Cocoa in the Florida State League for the 1966 season, team officials told the minority players we would have to work out our own living arrangements. They finally sent us to see a black gentleman who owned a local funeral parlor. He agreed to put us up for a few days, while other arrangements were made, and let us sleep in the viewing room, which was pretty creepy.

Then in 1969, after opening the season as the Astros starting left fielder, I was asked to sharpen my catching skills in the minor leagues when Johnny Edwards got off to a horrendous start. Being a team player, I agreed, although I didn't relish the thought of leaving the big show. I had worked too hard to get there.

Houston sent me down to Savannah on a fifteen-day assignment. When I got off the plane, I asked a cabdriver to take me to the team's hotel. "Why bother going to the trouble?" he said. "They won't let you stay there. It's for whites only."

Instead, the cabbie drove me to the ballpark. I actually had to sleep for several nights in the clubhouse, while team officials tried to find me housing in the area.

At no time during those two weeks in Savannah did I receive any communication from the parent club. I might as well have been sharpening my catching skills in Siberia. After the agreed-upon fifteen days came and went, I'd had enough. I was sick of the racism in Savannah and the neglect from Houston.

On the morning of the sixteenth day, I called Carol,

who was back in Los Angeles, and told her I was coming home. My flight to Los Angeles the next morning had a layover scheduled in Houston. Hub Kittle, the Savannah manager, begged me not to fly on from Houston without talking to someone with the big club. He called the parent club, and the next day, as I was changing planes at Hobby Airport in Houston, here came Tal Smith, the farm director.

Tal delivered a personal message from Astros GM Spec Richardson, namely, that I should be patient and hang tough and that I would be recalled to the majors, which I was—for two weeks.

The rest of 1969 I yo-yoed between Houston and Oklahoma City. Three weeks here, two weeks there, ten days here, a week there—it was a dizzying experience. Somehow I kept enough concentration to hit .408 at Oklahoma City.

At the end of the season, I was placed back on the major-league roster. But before I could get too excited about my prospects for the 1970 season, the Astros acquired veteran Tommy Davis, pushing me farther down the outfield pecking order.

Once again the odds seemed stacked against me. After such a disruptive, unsettling season in 1969, Carol and I sat down and had a long discussion that fall about my career possibilities. We finally reached the conclusion that if I could somehow stick it out for five seasons—the minimum time a major-leaguer needed to be eligible for pension benefits—we would leave the game with no regrets and plenty of gratitude for the whole experience. If need be, I could go to work as a technical illustrator. She could finish her college education and pursue a career in either fashion or art.

With my standing on the Houston depth chart as fifth outfielder, third catcher, and second first baseman, could I survive long enough to qualify for a big-league pension?

That was the $64,000 question.

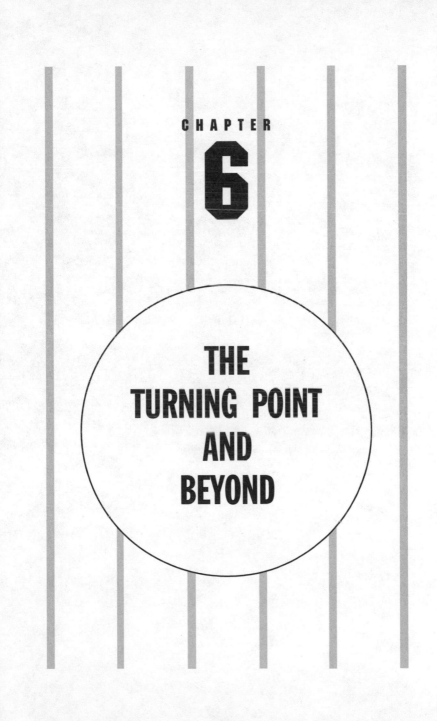

CHAPTER

6

THE
TURNING POINT
AND
BEYOND

The apprehensions Carol and I felt at the end of the 1969 season about my long-term prospects in major-league baseball were eased in 1970. That year proved to be a turning point, serving as the springboard for a big-league career that spanned another fourteen seasons and included appearances in two All-Star games and a World Series (New York versus Los Angeles in 1981) as well as the milestone of scoring the one-millionth run in baseball history.

I enjoyed a productive spring training in 1970 but left camp in Cocoa listed on the Astros roster as a utility man who could expect spot duty in the outfield, at first base, and behind the plate. My dream of being an every-day player continued to languish.

Little changed during the first ten weeks of the season. I had plenty of time to sit on the bench and contemplate the pending arrival of our first child. Carol was due to deliver in the middle of June, when the Astros were scheduled to be gone on a ten-day road trip to Philadelphia and Atlanta.

We were both anxious about the prospect of parenthood, and I was upset about having to miss the big event.

Carol calmed me down, however, by making a solemn promise that she would wait to have the baby until I returned from the road. Her assurance eased my worry. (As a first-time father, I was gullible enough to believe she had control over such things.)

When we arrived in Philadelphia, I learned a valuable lesson about always being prepared—physically, mentally, and spiritually—just in case your number is called.

In a curious twist of fate, Joe Pepitone, the former Yankee star who was Houston's starting first baseman, was arrested as we stepped off the plane in Philadelphia. He was handcuffed and whisked away for failure to make alimony payments.

Pepitone's abrupt departure pressed me into the starting lineup in Philadelphia, and I accepted the challenge. In the series at Connie Mack Stadium, I hit 1-for-4 each game and fielded the position cleanly.

The self-confidence that comes with seeing your name penciled into the lineup each night burst through in Atlanta. During the four-game series there, I lit up the Braves pitching for four homers—a couple of them game-winners—and 15 RBI. I delivered.

Then Carol did. When the team flew back home after the night game on June 21, she met me at Hobby Airport around 2 A.M. By the time we tracked down my luggage and drove to our apartment in southwest Houston, the clock read 3:30 A.M.

We tried to get some sleep, but two hours later she woke me up to say she was in labor. We gathered up a few things and drove straight to Methodist Hospital. At 11 A.M., June 22, 1970, our son, Keith, was born. He weighed more than eight pounds. On the same day, in the same hospital, under the care of the same doctor (Stan Connor), Angela Alou, the wife of my teammate Jesus Alou, gave birth to Jesus Alou Jr.

To celebrate the arrival of our son, and despite the fact I'd had precious little sleep, that night I went 4-for-4 against the Dodgers. For the first time in my career, I was named National League Player of the Week. It must have been the adrenaline associated with being a proud first-time father. (Our daughter, Kelley, was born on December 13, 1972, during the off-season. I couldn't celebrate her arrival with any hits.)

Within a week's time, Joe Pepitone got his legal affairs in order and returned to the club. He was ready to reclaim his starting position, but Astros manager Harry Walker refused to sit me down while my bat was smoking. Harry the Hat announced he was going to continue to start me at first base, news that didn't set too well with Mr. Pepitone.

Four days later, Joe Pep left the team in a fit of pique and subsequently was traded to the Chicago Cubs. I became the everyday first baseman for the Houston Astros for the remainder of that year and kept the job during the 1971 season.

Then in 1972, after the Astros engineered a blockbuster trade with Cincinnati that sent five players, including second baseman Joe Morgan, to the Reds in return for three players, including first baseman Lee May, I surrendered the position to the Big Bopper and moved back to left field.

I batted .312 in 1972 (fourth best in the National League) and again in 1973 (fifth best), making my first All-Star team the latter year. In 1974 I just missed a third consecutive .300 season, finishing with a .298 average.

My quest to reach .300 that year wasn't helped any by a bizarre occurrence late in the season against Cincinnati. In a game against the Reds, with my roommate Don Wilson pitching a no-hitter, I chased a fly ball into the left field corner, and while attempting to make a backhand catch, I plowed into the plywood wall.

The ball popped out of my glove and rolled free. By the time center fielder Cesar Cedeno could come over and retrieve it, the Cincinnati batter had circled the bases. On one pitch, Wilson lost both his no-hitter and the shutout.

The impact with the wall shattered my sunglasses, and shards of glass sliced and diced my face. I would need a total of seventy stitches—thirty-five over my right eye and thirty-five more below it. For several days my eye was bloodshot.

Adding insult to injury, Reds fans in the bleachers at Riverfront Stadium saw me lying dazed in the corner of the outfield and proceeded to pour beer and cola on me.

Looking back, I was fortunate that none of the glass flew into my eye. Otherwise, it might have been a career-ending play.

But despite that brief setback, consistency was becoming a byword for Bull Watson. You could pencil me in each spring for around a .300 average, somewhere in the high teens in homers (the Astrodome, with its deep fences, wasn't exactly paradise for a power hitter, meaning most of Houston's homers came on the road), and 90 to 100 RBI.

I was, as one sportswriter described me, an unsung hero in Houston. I went about my business quietly and efficiently, but with little fanfare. I was one of the breed of ballplayers who perform just beyond the arc of the spotlight. I never made waves, stirred up controversy, or called attention to myself. Basically, I let my bat do the talking.

My approach to hitting was calculated and applied. It went like this: Hit the pitcher's best fastball hard to right-center field. Adopting that strategy, I knew that if I was late with my swing I would hit the ball down the right field line. If I was early, I would pull the ball to left. That approach also allowed me, on off-speed pitches like curves, sliders, and change-ups, to pull the ball and keep it fair.

I refined a batting stroke that was ideal for the Astrodome. Fly balls were doomed, so I tried to hit hard line drives into the gaps in the outfield and hard ground balls that would shoot off the slick carpet and bound through the infield. Given the opportunity to play in some of today's ballparks, I'm sure I would have put up bigger power numbers (184 homers and 990 RBI in my career), but I had to adjust my stroke to the dimensions of the Astrodome.

I played on some decent teams in Houston during the 1970s, but we never could get to a championship level. For one thing, within our own division we had to deal with Cincinnati, the Big Red Machine that included Morgan, Pete Rose, Johnny Bench, and Tony Perez and was one of the best, deepest teams in baseball history. Later in the decade, Tommy Lasorda's Los Angeles Dodgers, with Steve Garvey, Ron Cey, Dusty Baker, and Reggie Smith, took control of the National League West.

Though Houston had some outstanding starting pitchers in J. R. Richard, Joe Niekro, and Larry Dierker (who will be taking over as Houston's manager in 1997), and some solid everyday players in guys like Jose Cruz, Cesar Cedeno, and Enos Cabell, we never quite had enough of everything to challenge for a title.

Besides making the most of the opportunity presented by Joe Pepitone's off-the-field problems in June 1970, I can cite one other, earlier, turning point in my career.

ANOTHER TURNING POINT

In September 1969, about the same time I was recalled from Oklahoma City and added to the Astros roster for the season's final month, Houston brought in Tommy Davis from Seattle in exchange for Sandy Valdespino. In Tommy, a two-time National League batting champion with the Dodgers, I found my own version of Professor Baseball.

Tommy was a walking encyclopedia on the art of hitting. He was a patient man, willing to oblige and indulge an aspiring .300 hitter like me who bombarded him with questions nonstop. Tommy was also a thoughtful and articulate man who could put his theories and concepts of hitting into plain, everyday language.

Unlike some superstar hitters who are geniuses wielding a thirty-four-ounce piece of lumber but who could no more explain how they managed to launch rockets into the bleachers than they could explain Newton's laws, Tommy had a gift for expression.

He could talk the technical parts of hitting—things

like keeping the hands back; the stride, weight distribution, and transfer during the swing; the position of your head—as well as the intuitive parts.

We talked for hours that September in the dugout and clubhouse, during BP (batting practice), on the plane, in the hotel. Morning, noon, and night we carried on a running dialogue. How to work a pitcher in the count. How to protect the plate with two strikes. How to recognize the way the opposing pitcher and catcher are trying to set up. What pitches to look for in certain situations, and so on.

Tommy kept a book on every pitcher in the league (both leagues, actually, since Seattle was an American League team). He knew pitchers' patterns, what locations they favored, and what their "out" pitch was. Tommy could get inside the head of the guy toeing the rubber sixty feet and six inches away and have a pretty good idea of what was coming next.

I tried to be a sponge, soaking up as much information as I could. I think it's important for any twenty-three year old, in any business he or she enters, to develop listening skills. If you ask smart people good questions, you can pretty much rely on getting good, solid, useful information. Some of the best advice I can offer young people coming up in their field is never, ever fall into the trap of being someone who loves to talk but hates to listen.

Tommy Davis spent the last month of the 1969 season and the first two months of the 1970 season with Houston before being traded to the Oakland A's. The time we spent together provided the cornerstone for my maturation as a big-league hitter. It also helped me realize and appreciate baseball's oral tradition, the way ballplayers pass along from generation to generation the tried-and-true methods for winning.

That oral tradition, sad to say, is disappearing from the game. Today's player doesn't spend as much time talking baseball with his teammates. Clubhouse games of checkers, dominoes, and cards, during which useful information and insights were exchanged amid all the bantering, have been replaced as daily entertainment with Walkmans and electronic games. Players today keep more to themselves. They don't socialize with one another as players did in earlier times. (On the other hand, they don't hang out at bars as much as we did, so the change hasn't been all bad.)

I can't say enough about the importance of the mentoring process in baseball, or life. There are any number of examples where students eager and willing to learn from their elders have received timeless, savvy counsel. Going back as far as amateur ball in Los Angeles (where I learned from Phil Pote and Chet Brewer) to the minor leagues (where Brock Davis, J. C. Hartman, Buddy Hancken, and Hub Kittle took me under their wings) to winter ball (where Tony Pacheco and Luis Aparicio gave me guidance and accelerated my education), I benefited greatly from a series of mentors.

Once I reached the major leagues, Houston manager Harry "the Hat" Walker served as my hitting mentor, and Astros coach Salty Parker tutored me on defense. Those two guys really helped me mature as a ballplayer.

I also made it a point to seek out advice and opinions from some of the best players in the game. Every time I had the opportunity during a season, at the ballpark before games, I'd talk baseball with guys like Billy Williams of the Chicago Cubs, Willie Stargell of the Pittsburgh Pirates, Willie Mays of the San Francisco Giants (and, at the end of his marvelous career, the New York Mets), and Joe Torre of the St. Louis Cardinals. These were smart, articulate, accomplished men whom I greatly admired. They all had valuable insights into the game that they were willing to share with someone who loved to listen.

In recent years, I think baseball has seen some great examples of mentoring in relationships like young George Brett in Kansas City working with Charlie Lau to refine his batting stroke, and young Don Mattingly coming up with the Yankees and being helped by Lou Piniella. I'd also like to think that during my tenure as hitting coach with the Oakland A's in the late 1980s, I

Myself, manager Joe Torre, and coach Chris Chambliss during the victory parade along New York's "Canyon of Heroes," Tuesday, October 29, 1996.

A full view of the ticker-tape parade. Fans from Little Leaguers to Wall Streeters filled lower Manhattan to celebrate the Bronx Bombers' first World Series title in eighteen years.

Joe and Ali Torre and myself and my wife, Carol, enjoying preparade festivities.

Standing in the general manager's box before the first game of the 1996 World Series.

Working at my desk in the New York Yankees office during the World Series. Official team roster boards hang on the walls.

Carol and I at the Roger Smith Hotel where we began the New Year of 1997.

Photo Courtesy of Alicia Eythewood

My daughter, Kelley's debutant reception in 1992 at the Ritz Carlton Hotel in Houston, Texas. Left to right: Kelley's escort, Ray Alton; Kelley; myself; my son, Keith; Carol; and Carol's mom, Ella Robinson.

As first baseman for the Yankees I pick off Oakland's Rickey Henderson during the third game of the American League play-offs, October 15, 1981.

I score for the Boston Red Sox in the eighth inning of a 1979 game against the Yankees.

I score major league baseball's one-millionth run on May 4, 1975.

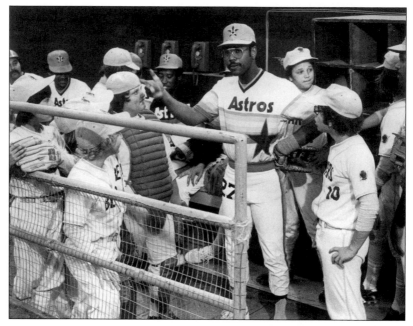

In 1975 I became an actor as a first baseman in the film, "The Bad News Bears Breaking Training."

I mashed the ball for a home run to the left field bleachers during a Dodgers vs. Astros game, April 23, 1978.

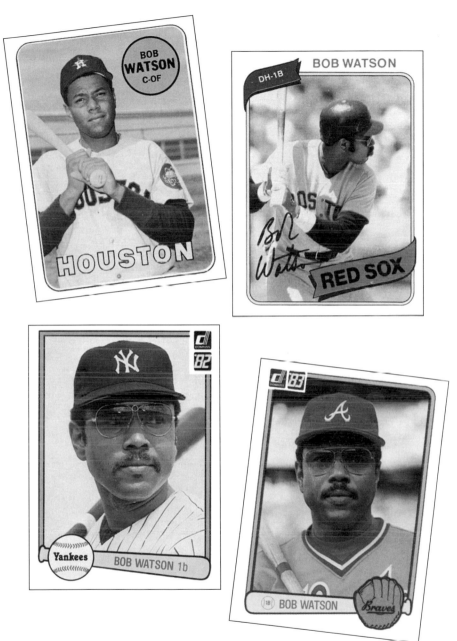

Baseball cards from the Houston Astros,
the Boston Red Sox, the New York Yankees, and the
Atlanta Braves. My career stats as a baseball player: Batting avg: .295;
Games 1832; At bats: 6185; Hits: 1826; Runs: 802; 2B: 307; 3B: 41; HR:
184; RBI: 989; Steals: 27; Walks: 653; SO: 796.

My family at the Astros spring training camp in the 1970s.

My son, Keith (4), and I as teammates in the Father and Son and Daughter Family Game at the Astrodome.

Carol and I are married on October 5, 1968, in Los Angeles, California.

had a hand in helping guys like Jose Canseco, Mark McGwire, and Terry Steinbach refine their techniques.

Another one of my mentors in baseball was Yogi Berra. People poke fun at Yogi for some of his famous malaprops ("half the game is 90 percent mental"), but, believe me, Yogi has as sharp and savvy a baseball mind as just about any I've come across. In addition, Yogi has an instant recall of his baseball experiences. He can see something developing on the field and relate it to an exact situation ten, twenty, or thirty years earlier. There isn't much that can possibly happen in a baseball game that Yogi hasn't seen or experienced—except maybe a twelve-year-old kid reaching out of the bleachers and grabbing a baseball during a play-off game. And besides that, he can explain why things happen as they do.

BANNER YEARS

My studious approach to hitting, uncompromising work ethic (begun those many years ago at Green Meadows), and unswerving self-belief—which was fortified by daily prayer and an active relationship with the Lord— helped me achieve some banner years in Houston during the mid-1970s.

In 1975—a disastrous season for the Houston Astros foreshadowed by the tragic death of starting pitcher Don

Wilson, a close friend going back as far as Los Angeles—I hit .324. I led the team in batting, homers, RBI, and game-winning hits and, for the first time, was voted Houston team MVP. I made the National League All-Star team for the second time and even threatened to win the batting title before an incident in early September in which I broke my right hand the moment my fist collided with a mandible.

I was twenty-nine, in my prime, and leading the National League with a .335 average. Nipping at my heels were Manny Sanguillen of the Pirates and Pete Rose and Joe Morgan of the Reds. Bill Madlock of the Cubs, who wound up having a torrid September and who won the title with a .354 average, was also in the chase.

The team flew back after a night game in Cincinnati that September and arrived home in the wee hours. Around 3 A.M., as I was cruising down South Braeswood toward our home, two guys in a Pontiac Firebird suddenly pulled up alongside my Chevy Blazer and tried to run me off the road.

They swerved at me several times. The first time I thought they were just a couple of drunks trying to weave their way home. I slowed down to stay out of their way. When they slowed, too, and swerved at me again, I realized they were looking to do me harm.

Things heated up in a hurry. When they pulled the Firebird in front of me and slammed on the brakes, forcing me to come to a complete stop, a confrontation was unavoidable. I didn't see either of them reaching for a gun or knife. I jumped out of the Blazer and decided to take them on. These guys had waved a red flag in front of the Bull. They were messing with a marine.

I raced right at the driver and before he could say a word, I smoked him with a right hand that landed squarely on his jaw. He went down in a heap, like a sack of flour. The other guy, coming around from the passenger side, saw his buddy lying on the ground, groaning, and stopped in his tracks. He looked like a deer frozen by headlights. Then he backed up a couple of steps and took off running down the street.

These guys weren't disgruntled Astros fans. They didn't know me from manager Bill Virdon. They were a couple of good old boys who saw a black guy driving alone down the street after midnight and thought they'd teach him a lesson. Only I was the one who did the teaching.

By the time I got home and told Carol what had gone down, my right hand had starting swelling. I had broken a knuckle on my little finger, what they call a "fighter's break." That injury cost me a shot at what would have been a career milestone, a National League batting crown. For a week or so, I tried playing with a light cast on the right hand, but I had lost my feel and stroke. My average dipped to .324 before I sat down for the final three weeks of the season.

My demeanor changed after that. I felt a smoldering anger toward bigots. I dwelled on memories of all the bad experiences with racism during my years coming up through the minor leagues. In the 1975 season I had come so close to attaining a major personal goal of mine, but because of racism, and my reaction to it, that opportunity had been forfeited.

Fortunately, I had the Lord to fall back on. He lifted some of the anger out of my heart. With his help, and Carol's, I learned a valuable lesson. I learned that I should have driven away, avoided the fight. I didn't—and it cost me dearly.

A PLAYER'S PRIME TIME

In 1976, I hit .313 and, for the first time in my career, reached the plateau of 100 RBI. My total for the season— 102—was the second highest in Houston history, behind the 107 that Jimmy Wynn, the Toy Cannon, put up in 1967.

Even the '76 season wasn't injury free, however. Prior to a game against St. Louis, I invited Reggie Smith, one of my buddies from the old neighborhood in Los Angeles, to dinner at our house. I was slicing fruit for a salad when the knife slipped and I gashed my left thumb, requiring six stitches.

In 1977, at age thirty-one, I had probably my best overall year in the majors, hitting .289 and setting career highs in both home runs (22) and RBI (110). The latter figure eclipsed Jim Wynn's team record and stayed on the books until Jeff Bagwell drove in 116 runs in 1994.

The late twenties and early thirties typically represent prime time for major-league hitters. That's when the mental side of the game or experience, if you will, catches up with the physical side to produce a batter's peak performance. Occasionally you'll see a player who reaches a peak level in his early twenties (Ken Griffey Jr., for example), and on rarer occasions you'll see someone peak in his late thirties (like Paul Molitor or Pete Rose, who remained a hitting marvel at forty years of age). But generally you can expect a batter's prime to fall somewhere between twenty-eight and thirty-two.

Injury cropped up again in 1978, the year I signed a two-year contract with the Astros and hired a lawyer, Tom Reich, to act as my agent in the negotiation. As I recall, I was the first Houston player to bring a third party into contract talks (which, I learned years later in a conversation with Tal Smith, wasn't exactly a thrill for management); up to that point, each player had worked out his own deal.

◆ S U R V I V E   T O   W I N ◆

This time I went on the shelf for eight weeks with a broken right thumb, courtesy of a wicked one-hopper to first base off the bat of Pittsburgh's John Milner. I played one week with the thumb wrapped up, thinking it was only a bad bruise, but ultimately tests showed that I had a hairline fracture. For the second consecutive season, my batting average was .289, but with all the time off, my power numbers fell to 14 homers and 79 RBI.

That would prove to be my final full year in an Astros uniform. Early in the 1979 season, Tal Smith, the Astros GM, came to me with two separate trade proposals: I could go to San Francisco in the National League or New York in the American League.

As a "ten and five" player, meaning I had ten years of service in the majors including the prior five consecutive years with the same club, I had the right to veto a trade. This was the basic player's right for which Curt Flood had fought (and ultimately won) in the courts in the early 1970s.

I weighed the two options and turned down both. I ruled out San Francisco because conditions at Candlestick Park (cold, damp, windy, and dreary) made it seem to me like a graveyard for hitters. Besides that, the mere thought of taking my thirty-three-year-old bones to that climate made me ache all over.

I vetoed New York because of what I knew went on inside the clubhouse. It was, as Sparky Lyle had so accurately stated, a Bronx Zoo. I knew all about Billy Martin's unpredictable behavior. I knew about his problems with alcohol and his propensity for getting into violent arguments, even fistfights, with his own players.

For someone like me, who took great pride in being a professional and acting like a professional, entering such a weird, bizarre baseball environment would have been unthinkable. I told myself, *No way, Robert Jose. You're not going to New York.*

Tal Smith finally came back with a deal that would ship me to Boston for pitchers Pete Ladd and Bobby Sprowl, plus some cash. I approved that trade and headed off to Beantown.

My first reaction to Boston was one of culture shock. Going from Houston, an expansion team that gained its franchise in 1962, to Boston, which had hosted major-league baseball forever, was like a musical company troupe leaving Peoria and going to Broadway.

The first day Carol and I were in Boston, looking around for a place to live, people on the street, including bus drivers and cabbies, were calling out to us. I remember one city bus driver opening the door and yelling out, "Hey, Watson, welcome to Baah-ston. You're going to love Fenway Paaahk."

This was my first exposure to a deep-seated, dyed-in-the-wool baseball culture. Unlike in Texas, where it's said there are two principal sports (football and spring football practice) and where I could have walked through Houston's Galleria scarcely being recognized, baseball is king in Boston. Because I played for the Red Sox, the pride of New England, I became a celebrity for the first time in my career.

Boston, less than a year removed from its painful play-off loss to New York (and Bucky Dent's home run) in 1978, still had the nucleus of a great team. The lineup included such stars as Fred Lynn, Jim Rice, Dewey Evans, Carlton Fisk, Butch Hobson, as well as Mr. Boston Red Sox himself, Carl Yazstremski. The pitching rotation included Mike Torrez and, long before he became a premier stopper, Dennis Eckersley.

I took an immediate liking to Boston, Boston fans, Fenway Park, and the Green Monster in left field. I hit .337 in 84 games, with 13 homers and 53 RBI. On September 15, on the road against Baltimore, I put my name in the major-league record books by becoming the first player to hit for the cycle—that is, to have a single, double, triple, and homer in the same game—in both leagues. Entering the 1997 season, that record remains on the books.

That day in Memorial Stadium, I hit for the cycle in exact order. My first plate appearance was a single, the second a double, and the third a triple (when Ken Singleton missed a diving catch). When I went to the plate for the fourth time, I knew exactly what I had to do: Go deep.

In one of the few times in my career when I consciously tried to jack one out of the yard and actually was successful—I tended to overswing in those situations, as most hitters do—I crushed an 0-2 pitch from Don Stanhouse into the last row of seats in left center field.

With Houston, I had hit for the cycle on June 24, 1977, against San Francisco, going 5-for-5 and getting the toughest hit, the triple, in my first at bat. Later, I got a single, a double, a homer, and another double, driving in a bunch of runs. My five hits tied a career high.

My spot in Boston's everyday lineup depended on Yaz: When he played left field, I played first base. When Yaz moved to first to rest his legs, I appeared as the designated hitter (DH), who bats for the pitcher. To be honest, though, I hated that role.

Being the DH is like pinch-hitting four or five times during a game: It's difficult to get into the flow of the game. Plus, as a starter, I always liked to keep a sweat going. That's hard to do when you're not out in the field, so I spent a lot of time back and forth between the dugout and clubhouse, where I rode a stationary bike, skipped rope, and hit Wiffle balls off a tee, just to keep a lather going.

As much as I disliked being the DH in Boston, I enjoyed great success in the role, hitting something like

.330 or .340. But I have to confess that, even though I've become a GM in the American League, which uses the DH rule, I think the game is much better off without designated hitters. I'd like to see the DH eliminated from baseball. Tomorrow would be fine.

I understand the DH's purpose. I know it has prolonged the careers of some of baseball's marquee names. But I'm a purist who wants to see the pitcher have to do the little things (like bunt) to stay in a game and wants to force the manager to have to manage.

Under manager Don Zimmer, with whom I developed a great rapport, the Red Sox won 91 games that year (more than any Astro team I'd ever played on). Unfortunately for Boston, Baltimore had one of its best seasons, winning 102 games for Earl Weaver; and Milwaukee, under George Bamberger, won 95 games, pushing us down to third in the American League East.

Carol and I leased a house in Wellesley, near the college, and we enjoyed our summer in New England. We had heard and read that Boston is one of the most racially divided cities in the United States, but we experienced none of the prejudice that dogged me during my minor-league stops. I suppose the citizens in Boston are color-blind when it comes to their beloved Red Sox.

The members of the Bosox were close and supportive. Through teammate Butch Hobson we were introduced to Marion and Edgar Sharp, who became good friends. Carol always marveled at the way the Sharps, who were from the South, grew collard greens in their backyard. Edgar also grew peppers, some of the hottest I've tasted.

We would have loved to have spent more summers in Boston, but the economics of baseball's free-agent system dictated otherwise. The two-year contract Tom Reich had negotiated for me with Houston expired at the end of the 1979 season. I was a free agent for 1980, meaning I could find the best deal available.

■

MOVING ON

In Boston a new ownership group, headed by former Red Sox player Haywood Sullivan, had purchased a majority interest from the Yawkey family. The new group, however, didn't have enough extra cash to engage in bidding for some of its key free agents. Consequently, I was among a group of players, including Lynn, Fisk, Hobson, Torrez, and Rick Burleson, who moved on to greener pastures after the '79 season.

Before choosing a new team, I spoke with the great Elston Howard, who had been the first African American to play for the New York Yankees and who, as an all-star catcher with a great batting stroke, had been one of the heroes of my youth. Elston, who was working in the front

office in New York, told me about plans to restructure
the Yankees for the 1980 season. The mercurial Billy
Martin was on the way out as manager, with Dick Howser
heading in. Yogi Berra was coming back to the Bronx as
bench coach, and the coaching staff would also include
Charlie Lau, Jeff Torborg, and Mike Ferraro. These were
all good baseball men, guys I knew and respected.

In November 1979, I signed a three-year contract cov-
ering the 1980-82 seasons. Carol and I relocated the family to Teaneck, New Jersey, where Keith and Kelley began
attending school. This looked to be a great place to finish my career.

It certainly was a faster-paced environment than we
were used to. On our first house-hunting trip to New
York, Carol and I flew down from Boston to LaGuardia.
We gathered up our bags and stood in a line to catch a
cab into Manhattan.

After a taxi pulled up at curbside and we climbed in,
the car lurched forward a couple of times, then stalled.
The driver couldn't get it to budge. As we wondered
what he would do next, one of New York's finest came
over and peered into the window. "Get this stupid hack
out of the way," he shouted at the driver. "And youse
two," he said to us, "get outta there, getcher stuff and
get in ta anudder cab."

Carol likes to say that's just the way things are in New

York and New Jersey: You need to stand up, shut up, or get out of the way.

We had a terrific team in New York in 1980, winning 103 games under Dick Howser. Reggie Jackson hit 41 home runs. Tommy John won 22 games. Rich "Goose" Gossage had a league-high 33 saves. Having started the season platooning at first base with Jim Spencer, I wound up getting most of the work. I hit a team-leading .307, with 13 homers and 68 RBI.

In the best-of-five American League play-offs, though, we ran into a buzz saw from America's heartland. Manager Jim Frey's Kansas City Royals, winners of 97 games themselves, shredded us in three straight games before falling to Philadelphia in six games in the 1980 World Series.

In the series opener at Kansas City, Larry Gura outpitched Ron Guidry, putting us in a one-game hole. The second game featured a pitchers' duel between Rudy May of the Yankees and Dennis Leonard of the Royals. Late in the game, Kansas City led 3-2 when Willie Randolph reached base with two outs, and then I drove a Leonard pitch off the wall.

The ball fell at the feet of center fielder Willie Wilson, who overthrew his cutoff man, U. L. Washington. But George Brett, backing up the play, grabbed the ball and gunned down Randolph, who was streaking for home.

Veteran Yankees fans will recall that George Steinbrenner went ballistic after the game. He was all over
third base coach Mike Ferraro for waving in Randolph
with Reggie Jackson coming up next. George obviously
thought Mr. October should have had a chance to do his
thing in the clutch.

Steinbrenner became so irate that he started ripping
Ferraro in front of players and the media. Dick Howser
finally grabbed George, pulled him into the visiting manager's office, and told him to cool it. George insisted he
was going to fire Ferraro, but Howser stuck up for his
coach. "If you do that," Howser said, "I'm out of here
too."

Trailing 2-0, we dropped the final game of the series
in New York, as George Brett hit a three-run homer in a
4-2 Kansas City win. Sure enough, Ferraro was subsequently dismissed, and Howser, as promised, left too. He
replaced Jim Frey in Kansas City during the '81 season.

That series was my first postseason experience after a
decade-plus in the major leagues. You always wonder how
you'll react to play-off pressure, when the heat gets
turned way up; and I passed the test, hitting .500 with six
hits in twelve at bats. I also learned a great lesson: The
best team doesn't always win.

The New York Yankees gained a measure of revenge
in 1981, the strike-shortened season, winning the American League pennant in two rounds of play-offs. After

outlasting Milwaukee in a tough five-game series (I hit .438), we swept three straight from the Oakland A's.

In the 1981 World Series against the Dodgers, we won the opening two games in New York then lost three in a row in Los Angeles before dropping the final game back home. The decisive game was the fifth, a 2-1 squeaker where late homers by Pedro Guerriero and Steve Yeager off of Ron Guidry were the difference.

One of my career highlights came in the series opener. In the bottom of the first inning I came up with two on against Dodgers left-hander Jerry Reuss, a former Houston teammate.

It was one of those matchups inside a game where I had a huge mental edge. I knew that I hit Jerry well, and he knew it too. Jerry threw me a sinker that didn't sink, and I hit a three-run shot. I hit another home run, off Fernando Valenzuela, in the third game. For the World Series, I hit .318 and had a team-high 7 RBI. But that was as close to a championship ring as I would get as a player. Along with die-hard Yankees fans, I'd have to wait another fifteen years before seeing that dream come true.

THE
ONE-MILLIONTH RUN

Despite a bid for a National League batting title, two All-Star Game appearances, and a couple of homers in the World Series with the Yankees, without question the most exposure I received as a major leaguer came back in 1975 while I was still with the Houston Astros when I scored the one-millionth run in major-league baseball history.

Fate, for whatever reason, once again looked my way. It was destiny, something over which I had little, if any, control.

By the beginning of the 1975 season, some baseball stats freak had pulled out a calculator and determined that the one-millionth run in major-league history would be scored early in the year. Tootsie Roll, the candy maker, and Seiko, the watch company, signed on as primary sponsors for a nationwide contest in which fans tried to guess which ballplayer would cross the plate for the historic one-millionth time and when and where the momentous event would occur. The winning fan and the player who accomplished the feat were supposed to receive ten thousand dollars (in the form of one million pennies), one million Tootsie Rolls, and a specially commissioned watch from Seiko.

The Astros were on a road trip to San Francisco in early May when the climax neared. The second game of our three-game weekend series with the Giants was rained out, so a doubleheader was set for Sunday at Candlestick Park, beginning at noon.

When we got to the ballpark that morning, we heard talk that the milestone would be reached that day—May 4, 1975. Given the time difference out on the West Coast, we concluded that someone would score the big run during one of the day games back on the East Coast, which were starting at least an hour ahead of us. No one gave the matter much more thought.

But as our game started, the big scoreboard at Candlestick Field flashed the number "10," meaning that 999,990 runs were in the books and only 10 were left to go. *Hmmmm. Wonder how soon it will happen?* we thought to ourselves.

The Astros quickly went down in order in the top half of the first inning. Ditto for San Francisco in the bottom. When I came out to lead off the second inning, I looked at the big board and saw the magic number had dropped to "3."

I was facing John "the Count" Montefusco, one of San Francisco's best pitchers. Montefusco had a sudden siege of wildness, walking me on four pitches. When I reached first base, I checked the outfield scoreboard again. The number hadn't changed.

Jose Cruz came up next and singled, advancing me to second base. As I made a turn around the bag and then stepped back toward the base, I saw the big number of the outfield scoreboard had dropped to "1."

Mercy, whoever scored next would become the answer to one of the great trivia questions in baseball! With games going on throughout the major leagues, there was no telling who that player might be. But, it dawned on me suddenly, I was one of a few who had a chance.

As I watched from second base, 180 feet away from history, up to the plate came Milt May, the Astros catcher. May went a couple of pitches into the count with Montefusco—*swing the bat, Milt,* I was saying to myself—then hit a rocket into the right field seats for a three-run homer. As I watched the ball fly out of the park, I could see in my peripheral vision that the giant "1" was still on the board.

At the same moment, half a nation away in Cincinnati, Reds shortstop Dave Concepcion hit a home run at Riverfront Stadium. He, too, saw a big "1" on the scoreboard and immediately took off in a dead sprint around the bases.

For some reason, perhaps rote, I started a normal jog around the base path after May's home run. But as I reached third base, I could hear my teammates in the visitors' bullpen, which at Candlestick Park was located down the third-base line, a short way beyond the dugout.

They were yelling at me to get on my horse and race home. Spurred by their screams, I ran as hard as I could from third base to home, touching the plate and stepping into history.

It was 12:32 in the afternoon. Later, someone told me I had crossed home plate a mere 1.5 seconds ahead of the hard-charging Dave Concepcion. Thank goodness the guys in the Astros bullpen had gotten me in gear, or I would have trotted my way right out of the record books.

To be honest, though, I didn't realize such a big deal would be made over baseball's one-millionth run. But a couple of hours later, between games of the double-header, representatives from major-league baseball came into our clubhouse and asked for my shoes and uniform, which they planned to send to the Baseball Hall of Fame and Museum in Cooperstown, New York.

Milt May's bat and the ball he launched into the bleachers were also retrieved and added to the collection of memorabilia. Check out the display if you ever make it up to Cooperstown.

That part was great. What wasn't so great was that I only had one pair of game shoes broken in. For the second game that Sunday I had to wear a new pair of shoes—and they left a couple of blisters on my feet.

I suppose that had I scored the one-millionth run as a member of the Yankees or Dodgers or perhaps the Chicago Cubs, I would have been able to capitalize on commercial opportunities. My fame would have lasted longer than fifteen minutes.

As it was, playing in Houston, which is somewhat off baseball's beaten path and definitely a long way from Madison Avenue, nothing much happened to raise my profile in the game. About the only thing out of the ordinary was, in the aftermath, my fan mail increased from ten letters a week to fifteen or twenty. I got a few more autograph requests, but that was about it.

The sponsors, though, did come through with nice prizes. I gave half of the one million Tootsie Rolls to the Boy Scouts of America and half to the Girl Scouts of America. After Commissioner Bowie Kuhn ruled that I couldn't keep the cash prize for myself, I donated the $10,000 to baseball's Retired Players Association.

I also received a handsome Seiko watch, a real keepsake, specially made for the occasion. It's something I'll always cherish. Not only that, Seiko gave each of my Houston teammates a commemorative watch. I'm especially glad the guys in the Astros bullpen got theirs; without them, that millionth run would have been scored by Dave Concepcion. And then his name could be tossed around at the bar when someone asks, "Say, who was it who scored baseball's millionth run?"

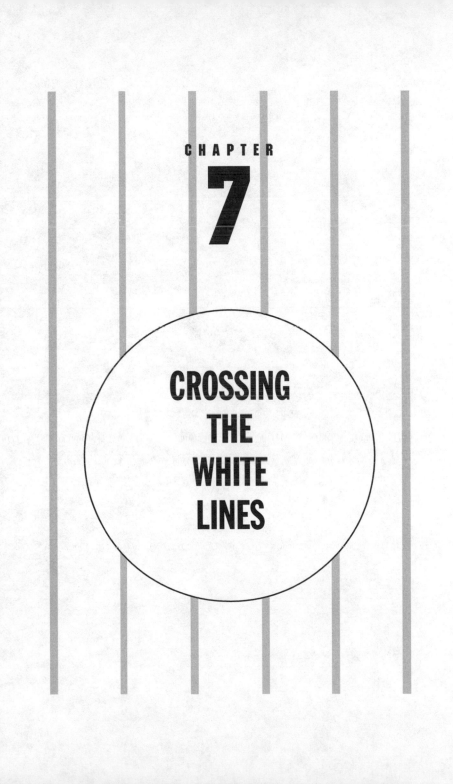

CHAPTER

7

CROSSING THE WHITE LINES

I spent the majority of my final three years as a player (1982-84) with the Atlanta Braves, having been traded there by New York in the second week of the '82 season for a minor-league pitching prospect named Peterson or Patterson. I can't say which for sure, mainly because he never made it to the big leagues and quickly dropped from sight.

My role revolved around being a platoon player at first base with another former Yankee, Chris Chambliss, and seeing more frequent duty as a pinch-hitter. Shortly after I arrived in Atlanta, however, first-year manager Joe Torre, who had come over from the New York Mets to replace Bobby Cox, expanded my role by naming me the team's unofficial assistant batting coach. Unofficial in the sense that I wasn't getting paid any extra money and wasn't formally designated a coach. Assistant in that Joe Torre also wore the hat as Atlanta's batting coach. But with all his managerial duties, Joe's time was spread a bit thin.

Joe had confidence in my ability and felt I could handle the task. He asked me specifically to work with the utility players, the nonstarters, by keeping them focused on hitting and prepared, physically and mentally, to come off the bench and pinch-hit.

Coaching my Atlanta teammates on the art of hitting was something with which I felt comfortable. As I've indicated, I had been a keen student of the art of hitting ever since I started out in Salisbury, devouring Ted Williams's bible on batsmanship. Now, all those countless conversations I'd had with Tommy Davis and other ballplayers were about to pay off. Joe Torre had presented me with an outlet through which I could express my enthusiasm and passion for hitting.

I was no stranger to the leadership responsibilities that came with being a coach. For my final four years with the Houston Astros I had been the team captain, a virtual coach on the field. I'd also shown the ability throughout my career to coach myself.

One important lesson I learned as hitting coach for the Atlanta Braves, which Joe reinforced, was to be flexible. All baseball players are different, which means that no single teaching technique works effectively across the board. A coach must have more than one way to impart his message, because different players will grasp concepts in different ways.

I don't care what sport you're talking about, a good coach, rather than having one pet theory that he or she applies to all players, learns to take each individual's natural ability and work within those parameters.

A batting coach works with players on fundamentals like the position of the hands and the stride. I also came up with some specific drills Atlanta players could work on using a batting tee, drills that helped them adapt to balls in different locations: high or low, outside or inside, or right down the middle.

Believe it or not, it's difficult to handle the pitch belt high, down the middle of the plate. That's why you see guys swing over it or under it, topping the pitch or popping it up. The reason it's so hard to handle is that players seldom practice hitting it.

I had virtually all the Atlanta players working with me before games. I devised a "toss" drill, where Braves players, using the team's indoor batting cage, would hit balls into a net. I'd toss balls to various locations, always making sure to end the drill by tossing them balls to the outside. I wanted to be sure they were keeping their eyes on the ball and arms fully extended.

I really believe in the value of repetition. Through repetition, hitting becomes a skill in which you're able to put your body on "automatic pilot." By that I mean a player's eyes will tell his hands, stride, and torso what they should be doing during the swing.

You see the ball and then hit it hard. That's it. See it, do it. There's no time for thinking about the process of swinging the bat, because a major-league pitch gets to the plate much too quickly. You may be thinking about the type of pitch you'll see next or its location or what this pitcher threw you in a previous at bat, but never about the swing itself.

Batting at the major-league level is all about muscle memory. See it, hit it. My friend Dr. Fran Pirozzolo, a noted authority on human performance, has a favorite saying for this: Practice makes permanence.

As a batting coach, I refined some of my teaching concepts and simplified the language I used. I spent a great deal of time working with Atlanta hitters on their self-talk. What a hitter says to himself as he steps into the box, whether his mental state is positive or negative, often determines the outcome of any given at bat.

If a hitter's self-talk is negative, if he's busy telling himself things that will create tension or stress (things like *Man, this guy's got his best stuff tonight* or *I never hit this guy well*), he significantly lowers his chances for having a good at bat. On the other hand, if his self-talk is positive, keeping him relaxed and confident, he'll raise his chances for success.

Besides needing to have flexibility, a good coach also has to exercise patience and honesty. Patience is required because changes in a batting stroke occur over time, not overnight. Honesty is essential because if you can't be candid with a student about strengths and weaknesses, you won't be able to achieve the optimum progress and development.

I remember working particularly hard with Brett Butler, a young outfielder with just enough pop in his bat to hit the occasional home run. Brett had a tendency to hit the ball in the air too much. I had to be honest with him and tell him to forget about power, that he had to take advantage of his greatest asset—speed—by learning to bunt the ball and hit it on the ground to the opposite side. To his credit, he worked hard and developed those skills.

Brett Butler, of course, went on to have an outstanding career with the Cleveland Indians and Los Angeles Dodgers. His inspiring comeback from cancer in 1996 is one of the most stirring stories in baseball.

The Atlanta hitters, particularly the bench guys, took to my coaching methods. In 1982, the Braves led baseball with a remarkable .412 pinch-hitting average. The next year, we hit a cumulative .389 in pinch-hitting roles. To post those averages as a unit is nothing short of sensational. Most clubs are hoping that their pinch hitters will bat something in the .250 or .260 range for a season.

By the beginning of 1983, my second year in a Braves uniform, Torre turned over all the hitting duties to me. Working with guys like Dale Murphy, Bob Horner, Claudell Washington, Glen Hubbard, Bruce Benedict,

Terry Harper, Jerry Royster, Rafael Ramirez, and Brett Butler represented a great learning experience for me as well.

The Braves had some good seasons in the early 1980s. With the proliferation of cable television across the country, which meant Atlanta's games were being broadcast to all parts of the country on Ted Turner's superstation, WTBS, the Braves developed a large national following. We'd go on road trips and find sizable assemblies of Braves fans, wearing Braves-logoed merchandise, waiting to greet us.

In 1982, Atlanta advanced to the division finals, losing a tough series to the Los Angeles Dodgers. The Braves won 89 games, the most in the Western Division, and Joe Torre was honored by the Associated Press as National League Manager of the Year.

In 1983, the Braves made a good run for the Western Division title again, winning 88 games, but finished second. Dale Murphy put up big numbers (36 homers, 121 RBI) and was named National League MVP for a second consecutive season.

In 1984, however, the Atlanta ball club started unraveling. By the end of the season, it was a foregone conclusion that Torre's tenure was over. (And, in fact, beginning with the 1985 season, Joe became a TV broadcaster for the California Angels. He stayed in the booth for five seasons before returning to the game as the St. Louis Cardinals' skipper in 1990.)

About the same time, I reached the humbling conclusion that my career was over. You can't fool Father Time, and I wasn't going to try to talk myself into thinking that at thirty-eight I still had enough bat speed to handle the fastballs I once feasted on.

After talking things over with Carol and the kids, I put out the word to Joe and the other coaches that I planned to announce my retirement at the end of the year. For the 1984 season, I hit only .212, and my career batting average, which at one point had climbed around the .300 plateau, wound up at .295. (It would have been nice to catch Joe Torre, who hit .297 for his career, but it wasn't meant to be.)

Joe had a surprise in store for me in the season finale against the San Diego Padres. A couple of hours before game time Joe said he was going to let me manage the club that day.

"What moves are you going to make?" he asked.

"I know one thing for sure," I responded. "I'm going to start myself at first base and bat in the third slot. If I get on base, I'm sending in Gerald Perry to pinch-run. These wheels are shot."

I played an uneventful top of the first inning in the field, then came to bat with two out in the bottom of the first. Greg Booker was on the mound for San Diego that day, and Terry Kennedy was behind the plate.

Just as it had happened with John Roseboro eighteen years earlier, when I came to the plate for my first major-league at bat, Terry Kennedy asked me what pitch I wanted to see. I guess he'd heard that day was my swan song.

"What do you want?" Kennedy said.

I stood outside the box, taking my time, looking down at Terry. "You know what," I said. "I've never asked for anything as a hitter. Just throw me what you want."

"Okay," said Kennedy as I stepped into the box and he squatted down and began flashing signs. "Here comes a slider."

Slider. The last pitch I hit in the major leagues was the same as the first. And, just as it happened the first time, when Junior Gilliam robbed me of a double, I scorched a ground ball.

Only this one went directly at the San Diego shortstop, who easily threw me out at first base. Without fanfare, I headed toward the Braves dugout, tipped my cap to the crowd, and motioned for Gerald Perry to take over at first base.

My playing career was history. That snake-infested swamp in Cocoa, where I first stepped on a professional field nineteen years earlier, seemed a hundred million miles away.

The funny thing about that day was that Joe Torre, true to his word, let me make all the managerial moves. I didn't go to the mound, sending instead pitching coach Bob Gibson when those situations came up. I did bring in closer Gene Garber to get the save. The Braves wound up winning the game, to finish 80-82, in a fourth-place tie in the National League West.

My ultrabrief career as a big-league skipper produced a 1-0 mark. It's safe to say that not many baseball managers can claim they went undefeated for a lifetime.

OFF THE FIELD

At the beginning of 1985, for the first time in two decades, I had no spring training camp to look forward to, no regular season to anticipate. Rather than sit back and start clipping coupons, though, I stayed busy by selling hard assets (gold, silver, diamonds, gemstones, coins, and the like).

I worked for Tom Cloud and Associates, calling on small pension funds and insurance companies that were trying to hedge a percentage of their portfolios against inflation. I wasn't a novice in the financial arena. During the summer of 1981, when baseball players went out on strike, I had served an apprenticeship on Wall Street with the firm of Cyrus J. Lawrence, working for the vice president of investment banking, Terry "Skip" Naglevoort. During that period, I began to broaden my reading tastes from strictly the *Sporting News* to include *Barron's, Fortune, Forbes,* and the *Wall Street Journal.*

As it happened, Skip Naglevoort was, and is, a big New York Yankees fan. He and his wife, Mary, were good friends with Yankees pitcher Tommy John and his wife, Sally. One night at Yankee Stadium, Carol wound up sitting next to the Naglevoorts in the box seats reserved for players' guests, and they formed an immediate bond.

Carol introduced me to the Naglevoorts after the game, and soon we began visiting Skip and Mary at their home in Wyckoff, New Jersey, and attending services at their church. On other occasions we'd get together with them at our home in Teaneck.

Skip shares my interest in baseball—and Jesus Christ. Since the early 1980s, he's been one of my prayer partners. We frequently get together for prayer sessions. We'll pray for guidance and direction or ask the Lord to bless upcoming family events. Or we'll simply give thanks to God.

Skip was instrumental in getting me involved with prayer breakfasts on Wall Street. These meetings, which rotate from securities firm to securities firm, are usually held on Wednesday mornings. People gather at 7 A.M. for a half hour or forty-five minutes of Scripture reading and prayer before heading off to their respective offices. I've met some wonderful Christian people, men and women, at those breakfasts.

The baseball strike of '81 lasted a total of fifty-one days, forty-eight of which I spent working at Cyrus J. Lawrence for Skip Naglevoort. Had the strike lasted much longer, I might have turned in my cleats and stayed down on Wall Street for good.

◼

A WIFE'S ADVICE: STAY IN THE GAME

Some of the best career advice I have ever received came at the end of 1984 and beginning of 1985, courtesy of Carol. She was adamant that I remain active, in some capacity, with major-league baseball. Night and day, she harped on the subject.

"Bob, don't walk away from baseball," Carol said. "It's been too big a part of your life. You've put too much of yourself into the game to leave it cold. Besides that, you love baseball. It's been your gift."

What was it that Garrett Morris used to say on those *Saturday Night Live* sketches? "Baseball has been berry berry good to me." Well, it had.

Looking back, I realize Carol's thinking was influenced by what had happened to her stepfather, Eddie Robinson. He'd had a long career in the music industry in Los Angeles, but somewhere in his late forties or early fifties, Eddie decided to make a switch and went into the liquor business.

The transition didn't go as smoothly as he hoped. He tried to get back in the music industry but discovered the doors were blocked. Eddie became distraught about his inability to resume his former career. Carol had monitored this situation closely and seen how deeply he'd been affected. She definitely didn't want the same thing to happen to her husband. Once was enough for her family.

Heeding Carol's advice, for which I can never thank her enough, prior to the 1985 season I interviewed with the Oakland A's to become their minor-league roving hitting instructor, a part-time position.

The opportunity with Oakland had been brought to my attention by the A's farm director, Karl Kuehl. Yes, the same Karl Kuehl who, as a Houston scout, had signed me out of junior college ball. (When people say baseball seems like one large family, I don't disagree. Over the years, my career has intersected with Karl Kuehl, Tal Smith, Joe Torre, and Don Zimmer at various times and places. It's funny how it works, but I'm sure it's part of God's plan.)

When I interviewed for the job with Oakland, I spoke with Sandy Alderson, the club's GM. I remember him asking me the question: "Bob, what is your ultimate goal in this business?"

I replied, "To be honest, Sandy, one day I want to be sitting in your chair."

That remark may have sounded offhand or glib, but I think it really did express a deep-seated desire simmering within my soul. If you're going to have a goal, aim high. And if you're going to attempt something, do it to the best of your ability.

As far back as the early 1970s, others had noticed my preparation and dedication to the game. Once, when the Braves were in Houston for a series, Atlanta team official Bill Lucas, who happened to be Hank Aaron's brother-in-law, said to me, "Bob, you should give some thought to getting into the front office when your playing days are over. You are just the kind of man baseball needs."

To hear that from Bill Lucas, who was handling many of the GM duties in Atlanta (though he didn't have the title) and who was the only minority executive in baseball in those days, gave me a boost in confidence. From time to time, even as an active player, I would think about Bill's comment and mull over my future in baseball.

BACK IN BASEBALL

I spent the summer of 1985 traveling to the A's farm teams in towns like Modesto, California; Madison, Wisconsin; Huntsville, Alabama; and Tacoma, Washington. Coming up through the A's organization in those days were terrific prospects like Jose Canseco, Mark McGwire, Walt Weiss, and Terry Steinbach.

These guys, even at such a tender, fuzzy-cheeked age, showed they had the potential to turn into the "Bash Brothers," who later won a World Series (1989) by sweeping the San Francisco Giants. They really took to the basics of hitting, going through the daily routines of hitting off a tee, doing soft toss, and working at improving their self-talk. They were eager, and they listened.

In 1986, I was promoted to major-league hitting instructor and bench coach for the A's. Carol, the kids, and I left Atlanta, a city we'd greatly enjoyed, and relocated to the Oakland Hills area of Oakland.

There I came under the tutelage of Tony La Russa. If you've read George Will's book *Men at Work* or if you keep up with baseball at all, you probably know about Tony's methodical approach to field managing. He was in the process of setting a new standard for having things buttoned up.

Tony was a really good communicator. He'd say what

he wanted to have happen—"giving direction," as he put it—and then he expected his players and coaches to follow through. He's a good delegator who allows his coaches to do a lot of the work, but he's a driven, hard-working man himself. He earns his paycheck, and then some.

What I learned from Tony were organizational and communication skills. I learned how to tell others exactly what I wanted done. I learned the importance of being accountable and following through, of not letting things drift or slide.

Tony changed the way games were being managed. He was totally hands-on, studying every nuance and detail, every single possibility for pitcher-hitter matchups in the late innings. He was the first manager to control the defense of the running game from the bench, by signaling his pitchers when to throw over, when to pitch out, and so on. He devised the "five series" for catchers to relay to pitchers, which meant you had to stay on your toes behind the plate.

During the course of a game, Tony really gets into the action. He has his bench coach feed him all sorts of statistical information about tendencies and matchups. He has coaches using stopwatches to time the pitcher's delivery to the plate and how fast players run between bases. He files away all this information and, sooner or later, pulls it out and uses it to win a ball game. All in all,

I have to think that Tony La Russa in the late 1980s took field managing to a higher level.

It was during the 1988 season, while I was working as bench coach for Tony and Mark McGwire was in the process of setting a rookie record for home runs (49), that Al Campanis, a veteran baseball man and member of the Dodgers front office, set off a firestorm with his disparaging comments about blacks in baseball.

Responding to questioning by Ted Koppel on the ABC news show *Nightline,* which was exploring the lack of minorities in executive positions in all of America's major sports, including baseball, Campanis said something to the effect that blacks lacked "certain necessities" to qualify for front office positions. Among those necessities, Campanis suggested, was intelligence.

People within baseball cringed at Al's ignorant and insensitive remarks. The sport suffered a black eye and immediately experienced a backlash from many segments of society. The NAACP, Rev. Jesse Jackson and his Rainbow Coalition, sports activist Dr. Harry Edwards—individuals and groups across the country—began pressuring baseball to change the status quo. After an accomplished career with the Dodgers, Campanis subsequently lost his job.

Even after the Campanis flap, major-league baseball as a whole failed to address the issue in a formal, organized way. Quietly, however, teams began searching for qualified minorities to move up in the organization.

Although many blacks, Latinos, and other minorities, including women, were subsequently hired, their jobs (accounting, marketing, ticket sales) were removed from the center of power. Fortunately for me, I was one of few given the chance to operate in an executive capacity.

While on a Caribbean cruise with my family after the 1988 World Series, which Oakland lost to Los Angeles in five games, I received a cablegram from Houston. Astros owner Dr. John McMullen and Bill Wood, the GM, wanted to talk to me about a job as the assistant GM.

I accepted the position Bill Wood offered on November 22, 1988, primarily because I relished the challenge of going into management. I had proved a success as hitting coach with Atlanta and Oakland and bench coach with the A's and probably was in line, sooner or later, for a manager's job. But I was more focused on finding a top job in the front office than a top job on the field. The goal I had expressed to Sandy Alderson about wanting to sit in a GM's chair one day seemed attainable after all.

By the beginning of the 1989 season, our family had moved back to Houston from Oakland. We found a townhouse on the west side of town not far from the residences of Tal Smith and Roger Clemens. Over the next four years, I was groomed in baseball administration.

My role initially focused on evaluating talent, both field and staff, evaluating facilities, and handling special assignments like evaluating players Houston was interested in acquiring. I was also responsible for our operations in the Caribbean.

My skills meshed nicely with those of Bill Wood, who was an administrator by training. He knew the business side of baseball, and I knew the competitive side. I also became involved with contract negotiations for players with zero to three years' service in the majors.

I began meeting with players' agents and hammering out the details. The first contract I handled in my new position was for Louie Meadows, a young Astros outfielder. I sat across the table from his agent, listening to this guy talk about Louie like he was the next Mickey Mantle or Willie Mays. As things turned out, Louie wasn't.

I'll admit to making my share of blunders in the job. I once cost the club about thirty thousand dollars because I failed to include the word *active* in a contract. This particular player's contract was supposed to provide for graduated payments for forty-five days spent on the active roster, sixty days on the active roster, ninety days, and so forth. Unfortunately, the player, a pitcher, became inactive after suffering an arm injury in spring training. We placed him on the disabled list, which was still the roster (albeit the inactive one). With the omission of the word *active* in his contract, however, the Astros were obligated to pay him at every forty-five-, sixty-, and ninety-day interval. He was, after all, on the roster. The GM and owner had failed to notice the missing word *active*, too, but it was my mistake; I should have caught it.

Believe me, after that experience I learned to go over contracts with a fine-tooth comb.

Carol and I were watching a program featuring bald eagles on the Discovery Channel one evening. The narrator explained that eagles teach their young to fly by pushing the eaglets out of the nest. Either they fly away or they fall flat on their beaks.

"You know, Bob," she remarked, "that's pretty much the same way it was for you when you became assistant GM. They pushed you out of the nest and said, 'Here you go. Fly or die.' "

"You've got that right," I said with a chuckle.

ASSISTANT GM

I arrived back in Houston just as a Texas legend, Nolan Ryan, was preparing to leave town. Ryan had become a free agent on November 1, 1988, and the Astros showed little inclination to re-sign a guy nearing his forty-second birthday to a seven-figure contract.

Two weeks after I was appointed assistant GM, Nolan

signed a free-agent contract with the upstate Texas Rangers of the American League. During the 1989 season, the Astros would catch plenty of flack from fans for failing to retain the services of baseball's all-time strikeout king. Astros fans attributed Ryan's departure to a lack of commitment by Houston's front office to field a winning team. The fact that Nolan was a local product, from nearby Alvin, added to the fans' disgust.

The criticism escalated after the move to Arlington rejuvenated Ryan's career. He won 16 games in 1989, made the All-Star team, and led the American League with 301 strikeouts. He subsequently pitched no-hitters in 1990 and 1991 (for a major-league record *seven* in his career). It was as if Nolan became the Ponce de León of baseball. He pitched like a pup into his mid-forties.

I doubt seriously any of those remarkable things would have happened had Nolan remained an Astro, however. A change of scenery was the tonic his career needed, and, revitalized, Ryan pushed himself into uncharted territory for power pitchers.

The Astros' attendance went into decline, dropping from 1.9 million in 1988 to 1.8 million in 1989, then plummeting to 1.3 million in 1990. When the 1991 team went a paltry 65-97, attendance dipped below 1.2 million.

By the early 1990s, John McMullen had developed a distaste for being owner of the team. He was constantly beat up in the press, had earned the reputation of a

miser after the snafu with Nolan Ryan and his decision
not to keep popular veteran Jose Cruz, and had further
incurred the fans' wrath by firing Gene Elston, the longtime "voice" of the Astros. On top of that, he had the
temerity to raise parking rates at the Astrodome.

I don't believe John liked the way baseball's labor
agreement was being negotiated either. He was a hard-
liner who would have liked to cut the players' union
down to size. When you add up all the body blows he'd
taken, it came as no surprise when John McMullen
tossed in the towel.

After a prolonged search, McMullen found a buyer
for his team in Drayton McLane, a hugely successful busi-
nessman, whose Texas-based food distribution company,
McLane and Company, is one of the largest of its kind.
Drayton's immense personal fortune, in part, reflects his
holdings of shares of stock in Wal-Mart Stores, of which
he is vice chairman of the board of directors.

Drayton took over the team in November 1992, creating new enthusiasm for Astros baseball. With a core
group of solid young players such as Ken Caminiti, Steve
Finley, Craig Biggio, and emerging superstar Jeff
Bagwell, the Astros' fortunes appeared to be on the up-
tick.

But first came a hiccup. The 1993 team, despite the
high-ticket acquisition of pitchers Greg Swindell and
Doug Drabek, a former Cy Young winner, finished third

in the National League West. Both guys had Texas ties—
Swindell had been a collegiate star at the University of
Texas, Drabek at the University of Houston—and each
had the potential to win 20 games.

Neither did. Swindell struggled to a 12-13 record,
while Drabek, victimized by a lack of run support, finished 9-18. The team went 85-77, four games better than
its 81-81 record in 1992. Given the substantially higher
payroll, such slight improvement was deemed unaccept-
able.

Someone had to be held accountable for Houston's
missing the play-offs, and the fall guys were, naturally,
the manager and GM. My close friend and former teammate, Art Howe, was let go as skipper, and the ax also fell
on Bill Wood.

Drayton called me in after the season ended and
asked if I thought I could handle the GM job. I felt ready
to meet the challenge. Plus, given the good young talent
on the major-league roster and with a strong farm system
in place, Houston clearly was a franchise ready to move
up.

"Let me talk to my adviser," I told him. "Then I'll
give you an answer." I called Carol, and we excitedly
discussed being on the threshold of our dream. We said a
prayer together and agreed to move forward. A couple of
hours later, I told Drayton he had his new GM.

On October 5, 1993, I became the first African-American GM in baseball history. If that weren't reason enough to have a party, Carol and I were celebrating our twenty-fifth wedding anniversary. As it turned out, we didn't have much time to celebrate that evening. Tied up by live appearances on TV news shows and lengthy interviews from the newspapers, we missed our dinner reservations.

Finally, Keith and Kelley got us some take-out Mexican food. We celebrated our anniversary and my promotion at home, eating enchiladas, chicken fajitas, and refried beans off Styrofoam plates.

My historic promotion was neither the top story on TV sportscasts that evening nor the lead item in the sports section the next day. Crowding it out was news that some minor-league baseball player was planning to retire and resume his basketball career.

Some fellow named Michael Jordan.

■

REBUILDING THE ASTROS

The rebuilding of the Astros was foremost on my mind in the fall of 1993. My first major move, made six weeks later, was to hire Terry Collins, the bullpen coach for the Pittsburgh Pirates, as Astros field manager.

I interviewed a field of fifteen to twenty candidates before narrowing the contenders to Terry and Bob

Boone. The committee making the final selection consisted of Drayton McLane; Bob McClaren, the head of
business operations (who is Drayton's nephew); Tal
Smith, a consultant to the club; Tim Helmuth, assistant
GM; and me. We had a split vote on the final ballot, but I
was pressing hard for Collins.

Drayton, who is a devout Christian, finally said,
"Let's have some prayer on the matter." He and I
stepped into a separate office, where we went over the
pros and cons one more time, then asked the Lord for
some guidance in our decision.

My prayers were answered. I got the man I wanted for
the job. In Terry, I saw a high-energy guy who had a great
feel for the game. Someone who'd been successful as a
minor-league manager for both Pittsburgh and Los Angeles. Someone who could motivate our young players.

The move produced the kind of results I expected.
Led by Jeff Bagwell, who would be named National
League MVP for 1994, the Astros were playing outstanding, aggressive, heads-up ball when the strike that
brought the season to an abrupt halt was called on August 12. With a record of 66-49, Houston was only a half-
game out of first place in the Central Division behind
Cincinnati.

Had it not been for the strike, I believe we would
have won the National League pennant and made Houston's first-ever appearance in the World Series. We had

great chemistry on the team, momentum on the field, and Bagwell was putting up Babe Ruth-type power numbers.

My first season as a baseball GM brought to mind that familiar refrain: What might have been?

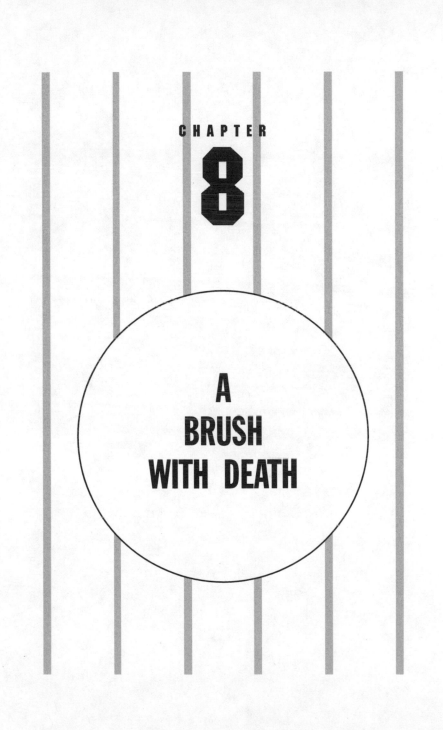

CHAPTER

8

A
BRUSH
WITH DEATH

With the strike over and training camp open, I was riding a personal high during the spring of 1994, full of anticipation about my first season as Houston's GM. Based on what I witnessed in Florida, I was convinced that the Astros, under manager Terry Collins, were going to bring excitement back to the Astrodome.

Little did I know I was about to encounter the biggest crisis of my life. I came face-to-face with the Big C: cancer.

We opened the season at home, against Montreal, and in front of a lively crowd of 43,438, beat the Expos 6-5 in twelve innings. Montreal, though, took the next two games, then gave way to the New York Mets, who came to Houston for a three-game series in which we won two games to square our season record at 3-3.

The morning of the final game of the Mets series, Sunday, April 10, we put the Astros players through extensive physicals at the Houston Medical Center. Many baseball clubs schedule team physicals during spring training, but with all the medical expertise available to us in Houston, we decided to wait until we returned from camp in Florida.

I was scheduled to take part, but because April 10 happened to be my forty-eighth birthday, I decided to pass. Hey, for the first time in my life, I was the boss. I could make a little time for myself. So instead of undergoing a battery of tests that Sunday, I took Carol out for a quiet brunch at one of our favorite restaurants.

I assured our team physician, Dr. Mike Feltovich, that once the team left town on a road trip, I'd come in and take care of business—which I did, a couple of weeks later.

During the physical, when it came time for Dr. Feltovich to check the prostate gland, a digital test that's no picnic, I remembered conversations I'd recently had about prostate cancer with two senior baseball scouts, Dick Hager of the Astros and Mel Didier of the Los Angeles Dodgers.

Both of these men had undergone successful prostate surgery. In the course of our conversations, each had mentioned to me a procedure called the PSA blood test. Dick and Mel said this was a virtually foolproof method for detecting prostate problems.

A blood test sounded infinitely better to me than the customary digital probe. As Dr. Feltovich was putting on that ominous glove, I told him I preferred taking a PSA test.

"You're way too young for that, Bob," he said. "That test's for older guys. Sixty, sixty-five, seventy."

"No, Doc, I do really want the PSA blood test," I insisted. I had read somewhere that black males are at greater risk for prostate problems than white males. I wanted to know for certain there was no problem.

"Let me just do it this way and get it over with," he said.

We haggled back and forth, as you might with a car salesman over price or with another GM over a ball-player. "Tell you what," I finally said, "if you'll give me the PSA blood test, I'll let you do your thing."

During his digital exam, Dr. Feltovich didn't detect any nodules on my prostate gland or anything else amiss or abnormal. But the results from the PSA blood test painted another picture.

A normal reading is 4.0. Mine came back slightly ele-vated, at 5.8. When I asked Dr. Feltovich what that read-ing indicated, he said it was a warning signal to run addi-tional tests.

So he made an appointment for me to see our team's urologist, Dr. Graham Guerriero. Dr. Guerriero put me through an ultrasound and did a biopsy in his office. He said results would be available in thirty-six hours.

Two days later, I was sitting in my office in the Astro-dome doing baseball business when I received a call from Dr. Feltovich's secretary.

"The doctor would like to speak to you," she said.

"Put him on."

"Bob, your physical was good and bad," he said.

"Give me the bad news first."

"No," he said. "Here's the good news. Everything looks pretty good. Your lungs are clear, your heart rate is normal, yadda-yadda-yadda . . ." He went on and on, avoiding the real issue.

"I don't like this," I said. "What's the bad news?"

"I want you to be here in my office at nine o'clock tomorrow morning. And bring your wife."

"Carol? Why does she have to come?"

"Just be here—and bring her," he said, hanging up.

My pulse rate shot skyward and my heart quickened. It's a comfortable 72 degrees inside the Astrodome at all times, but I suddenly broke out in a cold sweat. I called Carol and told her the news.

The next twenty-four hours proved to be a tough period, but not as difficult as the twenty-four hours we endured after we met with Dr. Feltovich and Dr. Guerriero at the Medical Center. That's when we found out about the cancer.

They were polite and professional and gave it to us gently, but they didn't sugarcoat anything. "Bob," said Dr. Feltovich, looking me in the eye, "you have cancer."

The last word had scarcely escaped his lips when I felt as though someone had put 200-pound weights on each of my shoulders. I slumped down in the chair.

The doctors told Carol and me that I had a form of

the most aggressive cancer going. Luckily, though, the cancer had been detected early. It was still encapsulated in the prostate gland, meaning it had not spread to the lymph nodes.

I sat there thinking to myself: *Why? Why now? Here I am, just getting started in my career as a baseball GM and now this?* Then I heard them say that they thought I might have as much as a six-month window before the cancer was likely to spread.

"Does that mean I can get through the baseball season?" I asked.

The doctors said that while I might be able to make it through the season without incident, that would be taking a huge risk. In their professional opinion, I needed to have the cancerous prostate gland removed as quickly as possible.

The next words out of my mouth were, "Well, in that case, who's the best person in the country to do the surgery?"

The doctors told me the top two specialists were affiliated with Johns Hopkins University in Baltimore and Washington University in St. Louis. Being a veteran National League man, I immediately leaned toward St. Louis.

A more compelling reason to choose St. Louis was that the prostate specialist there, Dr. Bill Catalona, was the gentleman who had invented the PSA blood test.

That gave Carol and me reassurance we were dealing with the best person possible.

The ride home from the Medical Center that day started off as one of the most somber and solemn experiences of my life. A million things went racing through my mind. Was I going to die? Had I been a good enough husband and father? Were my business affairs in order? Were the insurance premiums paid up?

One minute I was worried about my family's future. The next minute, I felt self-pity. *Why God?* I asked. *Why are you doing this to me?* The next minute I felt bitter and betrayed. *That's real nice. Put me in a position to take a team to the World Series and then pull the rug out from under my feet.*

But as we drove along, my mood began to brighten. I said to myself, *You're the first African-American GM in baseball, and now you have the opportunity to beat prostate cancer. If you do, what a spokesperson you can become. You can reach out to other men and become an advocate for PSA blood testing and early screening of prostate problems. You can make a difference. Do some good.*

Is that your plan, Lord? I asked. *Is that what you have in mind for me? Are you working through me to get the word out?*

When we got home, Carol and I went upstairs to the bedroom and stretched out. We held hands and talked things over. We said a prayer together.

Later that day I called Drayton McLane and Tal Smith, who had been named president of the Astros, and clued them in. They gave me their complete understanding and support. We began formulating a plan for a press conference to let everyone know what had happened.

Carol and I checked the schedule and saw that the Astros were scheduled for a road trip to St. Louis in early July. I called Dr. Catalona the next day and asked him if he could possibly work me into his schedule. He said he would be able to and promised to send me information about the procedure, including videos about the surgery and what I needed to do to prepare myself.

In the weeks ahead, we had another phone conversation in which he told me all the pros and cons of the surgery, including the incontinence and loss of erections, the negative things that men worry about. He suggested that I send some of my blood ahead to St. Louis, which I did.

I called a team meeting to tell the Astros players that I was having to undergo surgery for prostate cancer and would be out for three to four weeks. Then we held a press conference to announce to the baseball world that I would take a leave of absence during the summer and that Tim Helmuth would assume my duties.

Several reporters asked if anyone in my family had had prostate problems—my father, grandfather, uncles—and I told them I didn't know. We later found out that my father has an enlarged prostate, but it's not cancerous.

Carol and I did some checking into prostate cancer and learned that black males are 40 percent more susceptible than any other profile group. If someone in your family history has had prostate cancer, add another 20 percent to your risk factor. And, if you've ever lived in the San Francisco Bay area—as we did for three years with the Oakland A's—add another 10 percent on top of that. The San Francisco area has more cases of prostate cancer than anywhere in the world. As yet, no one has discovered why.

Our family traveled to St. Louis the first week of July full of confidence that the Lord would see us through. Carol and I told each other many times that surely the good Lord had a bigger plan for me than to become baseball's first black GM and then suddenly die of cancer.

I knew in my heart God wanted me to have more time on earth. Time to make a difference by inspiring other minorities to reach the upper echelon in baseball administration. Time to inspire other men, especially African Americans, to have their prostate checked out.

From the moment my illness was announced, hundreds of my friends, including ballplayers, went to have a PSA blood test. Their immediate response helped me see my own condition in a positive light. The anxiety and fear I had felt immediately after the diagnosis by Drs. Feltovich and Guerriero had started to recede. I believed

I was about to play an important role in publicizing prostate cancer. And I knew I had people from all walks of life, not just baseball, praying for me. More than that, I had a faith in God that had been built over the years.

CALM AMID THE CHAOS

At that moment, when my life was threatened, my faith kept me going. That same faith later held me through my first year as Yankees GM, when I felt pressure from the team's mandate to win. Recognizing that pressure points can pop up without warning, dealing with stress became, de facto, a part of the job description.

How does a GM stay centered and focused on daily duties amid swirling controversy and such intense scrutiny from without and within? How does he keep from letting the proverbial "hot seat" sear a hole in his britches? (Or how does a cancer patient remain calm despite the imminent surgery?)

I can't speak for other GMs, but I know where I'm anchored. My inner strength—a calm amid the chaos, so to speak—comes from my faith. Faith and trust in a loving God sustained me during the darkest hours of my illness.

I relate faith to being in the eye of a hurricane. While high winds and torrential rains are whipping everything in the vicinity, faith allows you to feel that you're in the center of the storm—the eye—where everything is relatively calm.

Faith allows you to see things clearly and unemotionally. You are able to withstand being buffeted by strong gusts or being bent out of shape like signposts or saplings. Faith provides you with peace and serenity to ride out the storm of life-threatening illness. It's the faith that Christians lean on to get them through a troubled day or night.

Although I didn't dedicate my life to Christ until I had reached adulthood, I grew up in a loving, caring Christian family that worshiped regularly. My maternal grandparents, Henry and Olsie Stewart, who raised me from birth, made sure that I attended church each Sunday. More often than not, I went to Sunday school class before the worship service.

While I wasn't immediately drawn to Christ as a youngster, having developed a tunnel vision for baseball at the age of eight, my grandparents instilled in me a strong sense of right and wrong. And with their help, no doubt, I was able to recognize the existence of a higher power in all our lives—a Creator—from whom blessings flow.

It wasn't until the early 1970s, when I was in my mid-twenties, that I accepted Jesus Christ as my Savior and dedicated my life to his service. The person to whom I give credit for this personal awakening and transformation is my wife, Carol.

In Houston she had become active in a Bible study group with wives of other Astros players and with some women from outside the ball club. She began taking a broader, deeper, and more active role in her relationship with Christ.

I could see him working through her life. Carol had always been a Christian, and as she grew in the Word, you could see his spirit filling her with wisdom and maturity—and bliss.

With Carol's example guiding me, I got down on my knees in front of her one day and pledged my life to him. My commitment to Christ strengthened our bond of marriage and the quality of our life together.

Carol and I had made sure that our children, Keith and Kelley, became aware early on about the spiritual side of life. We often prayed together as a family, and we attended church services regularly.

In the early 1970s, I had begun taking baby steps in my Christian walk. I began going out into the Houston community, as a baseball celebrity somewhat in demand, and giving witness and testimony. I spoke to businessmen, youth groups, kids in trouble, recovering alcoholics, church groups.

But perhaps the most meaningful Christian outreach I had undertaken came during the 1972-73 season when

I joined with three of my Houston teammates—Ken Forsch, Tom Griffin, and Dave Roberts—in setting up a chapel service for the team. These were nondenominational services where a handful of guys could come together to worship and give thanks to a higher power.

I'm not sure the chapel services helped the Astros play better baseball, but I do know the guys who attended became better people.

The chapel service we started in Houston took root, then spread around the National League. We began by setting up meeting rooms at hotels near the ballparks in various cities. Players like Don Kessinger, then with Chicago, were active in spreading the word.

I have to credit two driving forces for creating and sustaining baseball's chapel service: Watson Spoelstra, a longtime baseball writer for the *Detroit Free Press,* and Dave Swanson, who headed up the program in recent years before suffering a stroke.

Two decades since the inception of the chapel service, Bible study and prayer are now available to players and their wives on all major-league teams. Reflecting the power of God at work, the program now encompasses the minor leagues and has moved into Latin America. Baseball players are sharing their faith and testimony and spreading the word of the Lord.

This may not be widely known outside the clubhouse, but the '96 Yankees were a prayerful group. A large number of the players, including Joe Girardi, John Wetteland, Bernie Williams, Paul O'Neill, Mariano Rivera, Wade Boggs, and Derek Jeter, were committed to attending chapel services conducted by Rev. B. J. Weber.

I'm proud to have helped be a small seed for a program that has grown and flourished and touched many lives in such a positive, meaningful way.

Rather than preach a sermon, I try to live one. In my Christian walk, I hope others can see the presence of Jesus Christ as a guiding influence in my life. If someone asks me directly about my faith, I'm happy to discuss it. Otherwise, I leave preaching to professionals. Prayer, though, remains an important part of my existence. I take time each morning for a fifteen-minute daily devotional. Some people have a morning ritual of riding a stationary bike or working the *New York Times* crossword puzzle. My ritual is to set aside quiet moments for reflection and meditation. Sometimes I pray aloud. Other times I read from a book of Scriptures that Dave Swanson gave me a few years ago.

When Carol and I are together, which, because we maintain residences in three different cities, isn't as often as either of us would like, we frequently begin each day by praying together.

I know a lot of people do not pray regularly. Many people do not speak freely and directly to the Lord. All I can say, however, is that prayer provides a person's soul

with nourishment and sustenance and that God stands
ready, at all times, to listen.

He is someone with whom you can share a burden or
lighten a load. Many has been the time—at Houston
when I took over as GM, when I faced cancer surgery and
felt a bit overwhelmed, and later in New York when my
actions were being questioned and I was being held up
for public ridicule and scorn—I've turned to him in
need.

He's also there in good times. You don't have to pray
out of despair or despondency. You can pray out of glad-
ness or joy.

Besides my daily devotional, I find a calming reassur-
ance from friends with whom I pray—friends such as
Skip and Mary Naglevoort in New York, Roger and Katie
Allen in Oakland, and Dr. Fran Pirozzolo in Houston.
These people are prayer partners, Christians to whom I
can turn for comfort, solace, and direction.

When people in the media ask me about my religious
preference, I tell them it's nondenominational. Carol be-
longs to the Episcopal church in Houston, but when I'm
in New York or Tampa I attend services at various Baptist,
Presbyterian, and Methodist churches. I believe a church
affiliation is essential, because it feeds you with fellow-
ship and the Word. Religion is man's way of reaching
God, while spirituality is God's way of reaching man.

My relationship with Jesus Christ has broadened and

deepened through the years. It's seen me through some difficult times and circumstances.

I have faith that the Lord will be with me during whatever crisis I encounter. He will be there, helping me endure. And the good news is, he'll do the same thing for you. He certainly held me that July 6 of 1994, the day of my prostate surgery.

■

THAT LONG, LONG DAY OF SURGERY

The prostate surgery, a complicated and delicate procedure, began in the morning and lasted nearly six hours. I had the easy part; I was knocked out cold. Carol had the difficult job; waiting around a hospital while a loved one's in surgery is always wrenching.

Carol, Keith, and some of our closest friends were gathered in the waiting area, doing their best to be confident and upbeat. At times like that, faith pulls you through. Drayton McLane flew in from Houston to be with us. So did two of Carol's closest friends, Susie Paine and Judy McCoy, as well as Judy's husband, Rev. Joseph McCoy, who's a minister in Nashville.

Dr. Catalona and his team performed the surgery without complications. He informed Carol and me that my chances for complete recovery looked bright; the cancer had been caught in the nick of time.

I didn't realize that so many people around baseball cared about me. While I was recovering, I received phone calls, telegrams, and E-mail from all over the country.

My room at Barnes Hospital was covered wall-to-wall with floral arrangements, plants, balloons, teddy bears and other stuffed animals, and get-well cards. Carol and I quickly decided that we should share these gifts with other patients in the cancer ward, which we did.

Jack Buck, the well-known broadcaster who was the longtime voice of the St. Louis Cardinals, dropped by the room to visit and left me one of Jerry Seinfeld's books to read. He told Carol not to worry; nothing could stop a Bull.

We flew home several days later on Drayton McLane's jet, and I began the recovery phase. For the next two weeks, I spent more time at home than I had in years. I was not, as Carol can attest, a model patient. I got antsy just doing nothing.

By the beginning of August, roughly four weeks after the operation, I started going back to the office on a limited basis. I've no doubt Carol was ready to get me out of the house.

I was just getting back into the swing of things when the 1994 strike was called on August 12. With the Astrodome dark for the rest of the 1994 season, I had more time to regain my health.

In the aftermath of the cancer operation, I now undergo PSA blood tests every six months. My most recent readings have been .001—well below the line for concern.

I subsequently became an advocate for PSA blood tests. I had conversations with other GMs and team doctors during the '94 Winter Meetings and lobbied for the test to become a standard part of the physicals given to all major-league players.

I'm happy to say that my recommendation has since been adopted as policy. All ballplayers, regardless of their age, now receive PSA blood tests. In that way, I've been able to leave a small imprint on the game.

I also began serving as a spokesman for the National Cancer Institute. As part of a public information campaign, I posed for a poster with Stan Musial and Gen. Norman Schwarzkopf. All three of us are prostate cancer survivors.

As an advocate for PSA blood testing, I appeared with singer Robert Goulet on the *Today* show in the summer of 1996. Bryant Gumbel interviewed us on our experiences. We hoped to spread the word about early detection of prostate cancer to as broad an audience as possible.

Any males reading this book, especially African-

American men over the age of thirty, need to schedule an annual PSA blood test. I'd advise you to consult your personal physician. It can save your life. For more information about prostate cancer contact the American Cancer Society, the National Cancer Institute (addresses and phone numbers for both are provided in the back of this book), or talk to your local public health officials.

I don't know exactly what God has planned for my life. I do know that on a daily basis my goal is to honor him and serve him and be the best human being I can possibly be.

But I still don't think I've fulfilled what the Lord wants me to do on this earth. Yes, we've won a World Series, and yes, I've helped raise awareness of prostate cancer, but I have unfinished business.

I've been mentored, tutored, and talked to all my career, and I possess a strong desire, a yearning, to give something back to others. I would especially like to help young people realize their potential by giving them confidence that they can achieve their dreams.

I don't know what God has planned, but I believe he has messages for me to get across, whether today, tomorrow, next month, or next year. Messages about overcoming obstacles and persevering.

I can share those kinds of messages because I'm still standing. I made it. I survived.

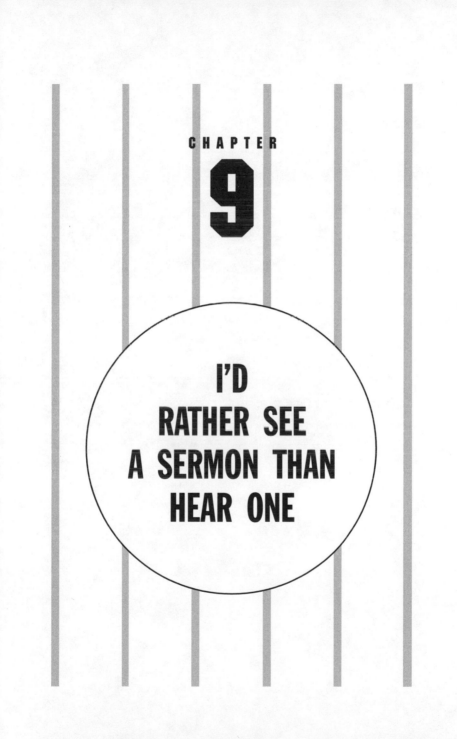

CHAPTER

9

I'D
RATHER SEE
A SERMON THAN
HEAR ONE

Jackie Robinson, with the encouragement and emotional support from Brooklyn GM Branch Rickey, broke through baseball's racial barrier in 1947. In the intervening half-century since Robinson had to endure hatred and hostility, even from his own teammates, some of baseball's biggest names have been African Americans.

I'm speaking of some remarkable athletes who performed under extreme pressure: all-time home-run king Hank Aaron, pitching whiz Bob Gibson, the incomparable Willie Mays, and the New York Yankees' own Reggie Jackson, Mr. October. The current generation of baseball's superstars counts blacks like Barry Bonds, Ken Griffey Jr., Frank Thomas, and Albert Belle among its ranks.

A large number of ballplayers in the major leagues during the 1996 season were either black or Latino. The legacy of Jackie Robinson's courageous career, moving baseball beyond its lily-white past and opening doors of opportunity for minority players, is alive and gloriously well.

Bob Watson broke the racial barrier to baseball's

executive suite in 1993. (You can make the case that Bill Lucas served as a de facto GM for Atlanta back in the early 1970s, but he never had the title.) I'll be curious to know as the next half-century unfolds how many other blacks will rise to positions of decision-making responsibility and authority.

To date, Bill White and Len Coleman are the only African Americans to have served as a league president. An all-star player with the St. Louis Cardinals and later a sterling radio and TV personality for the Yankees, Bill did a terrific job as president of the National League. He was understanding, honest, and fair, and he had an appreciation for how players thought.

Sometimes I wonder if more African-American league presidents like Bill White and Len Coleman, or more African-American GMs like Bob Watson, are in store for baseball's future. Or will I become nothing more than a historical fluke and statistical oddity? A one-of-a-kind GM—the one and only black to sit in the chair.

In the past decade or so, baseball has made noises about accelerating the front office advancement of blacks and other minorities. Yet, for all the good intentions expressed publicly and at league gatherings, I'd say progress has been made at a snail's pace. A slow snail, at that.

Minorities have made inroads at the field level, as managers and coaches. But decision-making jobs—those of farm director, scouting director, player personnel director, assistant GM, GM, team president—have been hard to come by.

I see a few minorities already in the pipeline who could be headed for larger responsibilities. For example, Dave Stewart, the former 20-game winner for the Oakland A's, is assistant to the GM in San Diego. Dave looks ready to step up to bigger things.

Dave Wilder is the farm director for the Chicago Cubs. Leland Maddox is head of scouting for the Pittsburgh Pirates. Omar Minaya is director of international and major-league scouting for the Texas Rangers. Doc Rodgers is director of baseball administration for the Cincinnati Reds. Cecil Cooper is farm director for the Milwaukee Brewers. All of these men have ascending careers in the front office.

There's also an African-American woman, Elaine Whittington Stewart, who handles contracts and player negotiations as assistant GM for the Boston Red Sox. (Whether a chauvinistic, good-old-boy game like baseball will allow a female GM remains to be seen.)

But that's barely a handful of people, and the last time I checked we had twenty-eight franchises and two more on the way in 1998.

MINORITIES AND MANAGEMENT

I hope and pray that my career in baseball administration—and what I've been fortunate to accomplish by
paying dues at every level and being helped along the
way by mentors—will inspire other young minorities to
get into the sport.

I won't say that getting to the GM's chair represents
an easy mountain for minorities to climb. It's out there
more like a Mount Everest, a formidable summit to be
scaled systematically, in small increments over time. But
it has been done once, and it can be done again.

I can't stress enough how important the promotion
of minorities to the top levels of the game is to baseball.
Ours is a country based on freedoms, such as freedom of
expression and freedom to worship. If you work in a
profession and devote your life to it, it's simply unthinkable that you would be denied an opportunity to rise to
the upper ranks of management.

If minorities are not even considered for management positions, a natural flow of talent and experience
isn't being tapped. Baseball is underemploying one of its
biggest assets. Beyond that, though, I believe that if people are educated and qualified, they have the right to
compete for front office jobs. Discriminating against
them because of race and heritage is unconscionable.

Someone has to give minorities the opportunity to show they can perform. Baseball needs more owners like John McMullen, who brought me into the Houston organization and said, "Bob, we're going to give you the opportunity to help us win games."

The bottom line in this business is winning. That's the fuel that drives the bus.

Teams want to win—right now. The economics of the game—the potential millions that come with winning championships, the huge salary structures needed just to be competitive—demand it. The stakes have never been higher. Teams, consequently, are going to try to put together the best possible management teams—from the front office on down.

As I set my goal as a baseball GM, I basically wanted to demonstrate that I know the difference between champions and also-rans. I wanted to draw on my experiences to mold a winning organization, top to bottom. But without the opportunity extended by owners like John McMullen, Drayton McLane, and George Steinbrenner, I would have never had the opportunity.

When I got the job of GM, I went about my business without a lot of fanfare. Phil Pote, my high school baseball coach, had a favorite saying that has remained with me through all these years: "Don't tell me a sermon; show me one."

Your actions will ultimately speak louder than your words, so get on with your business. *Show* people what you can do. Don't sit around talking about it. Talk is cheap.

If I aspire to be the best GM I can possibly be, I accomplish that goal by hiring the best talent available. White, black, red, pink, purple—the color of their skin, their religion, what they look like aren't what matter to me. I'm looking for people who perform . . . at every level of the organization.

Then I let them do their jobs, exercising the abilities they've developed and honed. If it's the manager, he manages. If it's the scout, he scouts. If it's the group sales director, he sells. Or she sells.

I can't prove my abilities as a GM by giving interviews to the press. Or speeches to my colleagues. Or by writing books like this one. I can only demonstrate my ability by bringing talent together, giving them the support—financial, emotional, spiritual, whatever it takes—and trusting them to perform at their best. You can't be a real leader without trust.

And you can't be a leader without innovations.

INNOVATIVE PROGRAMS

One of the innovations I've made as a baseball executive is the "Life Skills" program I initiated for the Houston Astros in 1989. Remembering training camps a quarter century earlier, when the Astros had buses going in and out of Cocoa like cattle cars and ballplayers felt like meat on the hoof, I decided to try to smooth the transition for young ballplayers, especially those from foreign countries.

I also drew on personal experiences in Salisbury and Savannah, where I felt ostracized and out of the loop. Acclimatization is important for any youngster, but especially to those who come to the United States from another country. It's hard enough to earn a job playing baseball when you are competing on your own soil. Imagine what it must be like for a kid from Venezuela, Puerto Rico, or the Dominican Republic who comes to a foreign country and faces a significant communications gap, not to mention a different culture. The experience can be overwhelming.

For example, one of our Yankees coaches, Jose Cardenal, a native of Cuba, told me that during his first summer playing baseball in America, he ate ham and eggs at every meal for three months. That's because those were the only two words he knew how to say in English.

With that as a reference point, I set up a program to help foreign ballplayers do normal, everyday things that Americans take for granted. Things like open a bank account, rent an apartment, apply for a driver's license, and order off a menu. We helped some players learn English as a second language.

The impact has been to give these young men a chance to live a reasonably normal life while they compete for a job in baseball. Now they have a better chance to survive the ordeal. In the intervening years, more and more major-league teams have started programs similar to "Life Skills."

REACH FOR THE STARS

Bill Wood, whom I credit for accelerating my learning curve in the front office, and I developed another innovative program in Houston called "Reach for the Stars," a one-year internship in which we hired an aspiring minority to learn all facets of the baseball business. The applicant we selected began working before spring training, then went through camp and spent the summer with our Class A minor-league affiliate.

The intern was rotated every few weeks through various departments, such as season-ticket sales, stadium operations, and advertising sales. He worked on the ground crew, worked with members of the scouting department, and attended scout school.

At the end of the year, if the intern wanted to stay in baseball, we tried to find an opening in our organization. If that wasn't possible, we took the intern to the Winter Meetings and introduced him to representatives of the 120 minor-league and 28 major-league teams. We tried to help the intern find a good fit and begin a career in baseball.

Unfortunately, after the strike in 1994 our "Reach for the Stars" program was a 1995 budget casualty. I plan to implement it with the Yankees, possibly as early as the 1998 season.

One of my personal goals for this year is to speak to the two league presidents about mandating a similar intern program throughout baseball. That way, rather than having one team like the Houston Astros moving forward in minority hiring, we would have thirty. It would represent a significant beginning.

THE TRULY GREAT PIONEERS

I don't want to leave the impression that I think my accomplishments in baseball administration can compare with Jackie Robinson's achievements in breaking baseball's color line. His big step for mankind eventually opened up all of professional sports to all races of people.

Jackie was a brave pioneer. So was Curt Flood, who courageously tested baseball's century-old reserve clause. Curt's decision not to accept a trade from St. Louis to Philadelphia after the 1969 season set in motion the system of free agency now in place.

Curt died January 20, 1997, a victim of throat cancer. He sacrificed his own career to do what he thought was right. In a letter to Commissioner Bowie Kuhn, Curt wrote, "I do not feel I am a piece of property to be bought and sold."

Flood took a severe hit financially and emotionally by sitting out the 1970 season. He was treated by baseball as a pariah (retiring after 1971) and never received the recognition he deserved for his courageous stand. Suffice it to say, every one of today's modern ballplayers owes him a debt of gratitude. As Joe Torre likes to remind his players, "So much of what you have is because of this man."

My story lacks the personal courage that Jackie Robinson and Curt Flood displayed. But it does show that a kid from the poor side of town, without an affluent upbringing or Ivy League education, can succeed in one of the toughest, most competitive environments in professional sports. An environment where you are judged—

rightly or wrongly, fairly or not—pretty much on the basis of your win-loss record. To succeed in such an arena, you'd better have a firm grasp of what it takes to become a champion.

CHAPTER

10

THE MAKING OF A CHAMPION

One of the people I most admire in the world of sports is Jack Nicklaus, the professional golfer, who has won more major golf championships (twenty) than anyone in history. At age forty-six, beyond his prime and given little chance to defeat younger competitors, Nicklaus won the Masters Tournament at Augusta National—for a record *sixth* time.

Although Jack Nicklaus was by far the longest driver of his generation and is, without question, the best clutch putter that golf has ever seen, I admire him more for his mental approach, his championship-caliber thinking.

Nicklaus exemplifies a champion's attitude. He plays his own game at all times. He controls his emotions, calculates his chances, and plays the percentages. He's strong-willed enough never to beat himself by taking foolish reckless chances. And he never, ever, gives up.

"Champions are made by risking more than others are willing to risk," Nicklaus once said. "Dreaming of more than others really think is practical. And expecting more than any others think is possible."

That observation embodies the creed I try to live by.

The message, in essence, is never set limits on yourself and don't let others impose boundaries on you. Stay true to yourself and your vision, be positive and persistent, and always forge ahead.

Years ago, when I started playing regularly in the Houston Astros lineup, I set a goal for myself of getting two hits each game. With that target, I believed, I'd make a big name for myself in major-league baseball.

Over time, though, I learned the folly of such thinking. I came to realize that a limited goal and attitude will produce limited results. Through the guidance of Tommy Davis and others, I came to see that each at bat is special and meaningful. Every one counts.

I learned not to become satisfied with a goal that could be easily attained. Why not set the goal at four or five hits a game? Why not go up to the plate every time with the goal of getting a hit—or at least having a good at bat?

I refocused my mental approach to try and make each at bat meaningful. This, I suppose, would be analogous to Jack Nicklaus taking a "one shot at a time" approach to the golf course, which no doubt he does.

Reality says, of course, that a major-league hitter will fail more often than not. If you're able to get 3 hits in 10 at bats—keep in mind, that's seven failures—you'll command a seven-figure salary and be set for life. Take that success ratio up to 3.5 hits in 10 appearances, and you'll have a good shot at making the cover of *Sports Illustrated* and the *Sporting News*. Go 4-for-10, and they'll reserve room for you at the Hall of Fame in Cooperstown.

Golf happens to be another sport where even the greatest players, like Jack Nicklaus, have to learn to adapt to defeat and learn from it. As dominant a player as Nicklaus was, he only won something like 10 percent of the PGA Tour events he entered and something like 15 percent of the majors. Yet his record is the best in the history of the game.

In baseball—or any other human endeavor—a winner's attitude is characterized by being systematic in approach, consistent in effort, and persistent in pursuit of excellence.

Speaking of persistence, Calvin Coolidge, the thirtieth president of the United States, once addressed the subject with such clarity that I keep his statement in a file folder in my office and refer to it from time to time.

Coolidge happened to be a reticent man, so averse to the politician's formula of saying twenty words (or thirty) when five will suffice that he was nicknamed "Silent Cal." When he declined to seek a second term in the Oval Office, Coolidge, with typical brevity, said, "I do not choose to run for president in 1928." That must have been the shortest press conference on record.

On one of those rare occasions when he felt chatty, however, Coolidge offered this observation: "Nothing in the world can take the place of persistence. Talent will not. There is nothing more common than unsuccessful men with talent. Genius will not. Unrewarded genius is almost a proverb. Education will not. The world is full of educated derelicts. Persistence and determination alone are omnipotent."

In other words, set your focus on a goal and never waver in your quest. Have a passion for your activity, learn everything you can that is relevant, pursue excellence, and do whatever it takes to succeed. You will find that your goals can be attained.

Another sports figure I admire is Lou Holtz, the former college football coach at Arkansas, Minnesota, and, most notably, Notre Dame. Holtz has an engaging personality, and he's so full of amusing anecdotes and funny one-liners that he can keep an audience in stitches. Holtz is an accomplished motivational speaker, as well, known for making profound remarks.

One of Lou Holtz's favorite sayings, which years ago I wrote down and memorized, goes like this: "Ability is what you are capable of doing. Motivation determines what you do. And attitude determines how well you do it."

What that means, basically, is that a person's, or a team's, mental approach (or attitude) is paramount in determining success. How much do you want to accomplish something? How committed are you? If you have the winner's attitude, you'll make the necessary preparations to succeed.

A winner's attitude is primarily what distinguishes superstars from other great athletes. Pitchers like Bob Gibson, Don Drysdale, Tom Seaver, and Whitey Ford, to name a few, had a mental approach that set them apart. Everyday players like Pete Rose, George Brett, Joe Morgan, Willie Mays, Roberto Clemente, and Henry Aaron, to cite a few others, had the same sort of consistency. They wanted to win, and they wanted to win day in and day out.

On the desk in my office at Yankee Stadium I keep two printed cards. One reads: "Tough times don't last, but tough people do," which was the title of Robert Schuller's best-selling book. The other reads: "Do your very best and believe in the Lord to bring you victory."

Having such inspirational words at your desk, cubicle, or primary place of conducting business keeps you in a positive frame of mind. While shuffling papers or signing correspondence, you glance at those sayings so often the message enters your subconscious. That keeps you motivated and upbeat.

Possessing a winner's attitude also helps leaders exercise their ability to lead. In my mind, being a leader entails being accountable for your actions—to yourself, to your boss, and, on a spiritual level, to God—being flexible and adaptable, and keeping an open mind to suggestions for how to improve.

A leader isn't a know-it-all. Rather, a leader is someone who seeks the advice, counsel, and wisdom of others and incorporates those thoughts and ideas into an overall strategy.

Leaders allow people to do the jobs they were hired to do, such as letting Joe Torre and his staff run the ball club day-to-day. As GM, I wasn't about to tell Chris Chambliss how to teach hitting or Willie Randolph how to teach infield play or giving signs or tell Mel Stottlemyre how to work with his pitchers.

A crucial part of leadership, in my estimation, is accepting adversity as part of the game, or part of life. Rather than waste time and energy by magnifying an adverse situation, or dwelling on it, or seeking sympathy because it has occurred, leaders will resolve to overcome it—then get to work.

Leaders cannot show panic or fall apart in a crisis. Even though they might be concerned about a potentially disastrous situation, leaders must keep calm and centered. They have to set an example for others to follow. It's been my experience that a cool head handles a tense situation better than a hot one.

When the Yankees' comfortable twelve-game lead in July dipped to three games in September, my staff in the front office and Joe Torre's staff on the field didn't overreact. Players are always looking for panic or fright, and when they see anxiety and fear, they are going to feel the same way. That's only natural.

The Yankees players, however, saw none of that. To a man, we didn't panic. We talked about the situation throughout the crisis in September, and we kept our chins up and our eyes wide open. Our demeanors didn't change. We held fast, even as others outside the organization were predicting our imminent collapse. That same coolness, I might add, helped us overcome the two-game deficit to Atlanta in the World Series.

And people who were not seen on television those days also contributed to our World Series win.

YANKEE TEAMWORK

Yankees-brand teamwork means that the last guy on the roster is as valued, and crucial to the team's overall success, as the starting lineup. Teamwork means the role players, who seldom get any ink or TV time and who tend to be overlooked in the big picture, are as appreciated for their performance and contribution as the stars.

I can point to important contributions from every player who put on a Yankees uniform in 1996. Guys like Jim Leyritz, who filled in at several spots in the lineup and became Andy Pettitte's regular catcher; Andy Fox, an infielder who spot-started and helped us with late-game defense; Luis Sojo, whom we got off waivers from Seattle and who came up big on several occasions; Ruben Rivera, a rising star who made spectacular outfield catches to save wins over Detroit and Seattle and who got a crucial extra-inning hit to beat Baltimore late in the year; Charlie Hayes, who came over from Pittsburgh in late August and delivered a series of clutch hits and clutch defensive plays; Mike Aldrete, who came over from California, gave us an experienced left-handed pinch-hitter and got some clutch pinch-hits; Matt Howard, who played mostly as a defensive replacement.

Each of them helped us win games. The same goes for unheralded guys on the pitching staff like Jim Mecir, who saved a big win for us in late April at Baltimore when we were opening our lead; Jeff Nelson, who made more than seventy appearances in long relief and was a steady hand throughout; Dale Polley, who came up from the minors to give us left-handed relief pitching after we released Steve Howe; Dave Pavlas, who earned us an important win; Mariano Mendoza, who won a big game for us against Cleveland late in the year.

The 1996 Yankees also benefited greatly from the unstinting efforts of many individuals behind the scenes. Their names never showed up in a box score, but they were invaluable nevertheless.

Our entire medical staff, including team physician

Stuart Hershon, trainers Gene Monahan and Steve Don-
ohue, and strength coach Paul Mastropasqua, worked
overtime all year and did a great job keeping Yankees
players on the field. Stu headed the team that diagnosed
and corrected the aneurysm in David Cone's shoulder.
He also helped Graeme Lloyd work through his elbow
problems late in the season.

All baseball teams have to contend with injury and
illness during the long season. We were fortunate to lose
so few players for any extended period. If you look at the
1996 total at bats for guys like Tino Martinez (595),
Derek Jeter (582), Bernie Williams (551), and Paul
O'Neill (546), you'll see that many of our starters were in
the lineup from opening day right through to the end of
the season. That kind of relative health for a lineup gives
a team consistency and continuity.

We also received a significant boost from sports psychologist Dr. Fran Pirozzolo, who had worked for me in
Houston with the Astros. Fran had a huge impact on the
mental approach of the '96 Yankees. He made periodic
visits beginning in spring training and was with us down
the stretch and during the play-offs.

Fran, who is a good friend and a brother in Christ,
served as a calming influence as pressures mounted late
in the season. On a personal level, he helped me withstand the pounding I was taking in the press after the

David Weathers and Graeme Lloyd trades. He helped me keep my feet on the ground and my eyes toward heaven.

Fran also provided a strong shoulder for Joe Torre to lean on while he grieved for one brother, Rocco, who passed away from a heart attack in June, and during Joe's anxious moments in August and September when his one surviving brother, Frank, awaited a heart transplant.

I had seen how much a sports psychologist could add to a sports team during Oakland's heyday in the late 1980s. Dr. Harvey Dorfman, who now works for the Florida Marlins, had played an instrumental, though behind-the-scenes, role with the A's.

I can't say enough about how much Fran Pirozzolo contributed to the Yankees' success. He helped players with the mental and spiritual components of their game by functioning, more than anything else, as a confidant and best friend.

A winner's attitude. Leadership. Teamwork. When those intangibles are present on the field, and in the clubhouse and front office, success can be imminent. The final piece of the puzzle for making a champion, though, is having an outstanding work ethic.

THE YANKEE WORK ETHIC

Putting in a hard day's work is something Joe Torre stressed to the squad from the beginning of camp. He told players we wanted them to feel tired at the end of practice or the end of a game. If they're not, if they are ready to go to dinner or out on the town feeling fresh, then they have shortchanged themselves—and their teammates.

If someone is playing a hustling, heads-up style of baseball, he should be somewhat tired—mentally and physically—when the day is done. If that's not the case, however, a player should take it upon himself to get in some extra batting practice, fielding practice, running, or conditioning work.

One of the major criticisms of ballplayers in this era of megacontracts is that the work ethic has been compromised. Some critics contend there's an emerging breed of professional athlete who, with financial security and comfort, doesn't extend total effort or doesn't work to improve his skills as his predecessors did.

I'll admit that you do see a few slackers at the major-league level. There are some ballplayers, though not that many, who squander their ability by just going through the motions. In my career I saw a few guys, including teammates, who never put in the effort to be the best they could be.

I've said this before: When the best players on your team are also the hardest workers, you have a combination that won't quit. Our best players worked hard last year, and so did our role players. Basically, everyone fulfilled the commitment to his teammates to give his best effort.

By the way, I'm not overlooking talent as a factor in the creation of a champion. Talent, it almost goes without saying, is crucial to the mix. You can have a roster of motivated, mentally tough, and fundamentally sound ballplayers and still fail to win titles—if you lack ability. Any team, in any sport, has to have some big horses to saddle up and ride, some big guns to fire.

Yet I think most people outside professional sports would be surprised at how thin the margins of difference are in talent among the top handful of teams. Talent tends to get spread around; rarely do you see it stockpiled in one location.

The 1996 Yankees had their share of talent on the field, of course. Derek Jeter, our rookie shortstop, showed terrific presence and poise, and his selection as Rookie of the Year was a no-brainer. Bernie Williams, our center fielder, had a breakthrough season and stamped himself as a major star. Tino Martinez, slow start and all, drove home 117 runs. Wade Boggs hit over .300 for the umpteenth time in his career. Cecil Fielder came over from Detroit and kept producing runs.

Among pitchers, Andy Pettitte emerged as the ace of the staff and won 21 games, leading the American League. David Cone was having a typically outstanding season when he went down in May, and his return to the rotation in September gave the team an enormous lift. Dwight Gooden pitched a dazzling no-hitter in May and won 11 games in a comeback season. Jimmy Key and Kenny Rogers each overcame health problems enough to win 12 games. In the bullpen, the tandem of Mariano Rivera setting up and John Wetteland closing was like a 1-2 knockout combination. They put more guys to sleep than Sominex.

Talent? Yes, the 1996 New York Yankees definitely had some talent on the roster. But when the season began you didn't hear people refer to us as the best team in baseball, which we became. (I note that one national publication rates us the *seventh*-best team entering the 1997 season.)

I submit that the Yankees' success can be attributed less to talent than to our players' consistently displaying a winner's attitude, leadership, teamwork, and work ethic. Take those basic ingredients—add good fortune and some savvy roster moves and trades—and you have the makings of a world champion.

Which, by the grace of God, we became.

CHAPTER

11

EVERYONE LOVES A WINNER . . . AND A PARADE

On October 29, 1996, three days after the World Series ended, New Yorkers poured out their love and affection for the Yankees once again, staging a massive ticker-tape parade through the streets of Manhattan.

A crowd conservatively estimated at three million people, many sporting Yankees caps, jerseys, and warm-up jackets, turned out on a bright, sun-splashed Tuesday morning to hail their conquering heroes. Schoolchildren played hooky to pay homage, and businesspeople wearing—what else?—pin-striped suits blew off their appointments.

Hours before the parade, people began lining up. Spontaneous chants of "Let's Go Yankees" broke out up and down the boulevard. No one wanted to miss the Yankees' victory fete, which began around 11:30 A.M. and rapidly took on the massive proportions of a celebration at the end of a foreign war. Some people pegged the parade as the largest since troops came home from the Persian Gulf War in 1991. Other observers said you had to go all the way back to 1951, when Gen. Douglas MacArthur came back from Korea.

Players, team officials, and assorted dignitaries rode

on specially designed floats, waving at fans lined up fifteen to twenty people deep along the parade route,
which extended from Battery Park up Broadway to City
Hall. Joe Torre, ever the team leader, rode on the front
float with his coaching staff. Fittingly, John Wetteland
and Mariano Rivera were at the end of the procession.
The closers.

Accompanying the fifty to sixty floats and con-
vertibles was everyone from the famed Radio City Music
Hall's Rockettes (bedecked in green Christmas skirts and
Santa caps) and bands and cheerleading squads from
local high schools to a delegation of three hundred parents and children proudly carrying the colors of the Joe
Torre East Highway Little League in Brooklyn.

"For a city the size of New York to take on that small-
town feel, it was like Main Street, U.S.A.," Torre would
observe. "You see it all the time, but not in New York
City. To have this kind of support is mind-boggling."

Mind-boggling, indeed. Pennants, banners, and
streamers bearing the Yankees insignia hung from street
signs and were unfurled from windows in office build-
ings. Fans on the street flashed homemade signs ex-
tolling the world champions and the masterful field
manager whose family had captured their hearts:

Joe Torre for President.

Joe, You'll Go Down in His-Torre!

Many hearts, though, were reserved for rookie shortstop Derek Jeter. The parade couldn't proceed half a block without the heartthrob passing signs reading:

I Love You, Derek!

Derek, Will You Marry Me?

We Played Hookie [sic] to See Our Rookie!

The scene was surreal. It was as though the skies had opened and poured out a paper blizzard. Computer paper, fax paper, toilet paper, newspaper, telephone book pages: The sky was filled with white paper. New York sanitation crews later estimated they cleaned up between seventy-five and one hundred *tons* of paper.

And it was loud. So deafeningly loud that earplugs given to the Yankees players proved to be of little use. "The decibel level had to be more than a 747 taking off," said third baseman Wade Boggs. "It was a constant roar. You couldn't talk to the guy who was standing next to you. You couldn't hear."

"They [the Yankees fans] were so loud my ears were ringing," echoed catcher Joe Girardi. "The decibel level was incredible. If you measured it with one of those noise meters, it was probably unhealthy."

But the scene was safe. Unlike celebrations for sports championships in other major cities, where rioting and looting often are part of the package, the victory parade produced neither vandalism nor rowdiness. City police reported making only a handful of arrests for minor disturbances.

Some New Yorkers seemed amazed by that statistic, but all anyone could see on the streets of Manhattan, for blocks and blocks and miles and miles, were smiles. Big, wide, toothy, ear-to-ear smiles.

The Yankees' victory parade was a virtual lovefest, an outpouring of emotion for a never-say-die ball club whose resiliency and resoluteness had finally won over the skeptics and naysayers. One New York columnist described the parade as a "Woodstock for baseball fans." Another called it a "gigantic love-in that made Woodstock look like a penal colony."

At the end of the parade route, city officials, including Mayor Rudy Giuliani, who along with his son, Andrew, had ridden in the parade, introduced the Yankees players on a special platform set up on City Hall Plaza. What ensued was a celebration that lasted well into the afternoon. Which was fine with all concerned, because no one was in a hurry for the party to end.

There eight-year-old Christina Skleros began the ceremony by singing the national anthem, as she had done before game six of the World Series. There opera star Placido Domingo sang "Take Me Out to the Ball Game," and perennial New York favorite Robert Merrill sang "America the Beautiful."

There Mayor Giuliani declared, "The New York Yankees are the greatest franchise in sports, and this city is the greatest city in the world." Giuliani, who would present to each member of the Yankees a key to the city, also said, "Like New Yorkers, this team plays better under pressure."

There New York Governor George Pataki, who rode along the parade route in a convertible, seated next to the legendary Joe DiMaggio, said, "I think that George Steinbrenner realizes there's no other place to be than in New York"—a reference to the possibility the team might relocate after its lease in the Bronx expires in 2002. "When you think about the Yankees, you think about New York. They're going to be here forever."

Governor Pataki added, "There's no place worth winning, unless it's New York. This is the best."

There Wade Boggs, who had ridden horseback with one of New York's finest during the postgame celebration at Yankee Stadium, received a mounted policeman's helmet from Police Commissioner Howard Safir. "I'm so proud to be a Yankee," said the ebullient Boggs. "But most of all, I'm so proud of you fans. That parade was the greatest spectacle ever in the history of sports."

There George Steinbrenner and Joe DiMaggio presented Mayor Giuliani with the World Series trophy, which will be displayed at City Hall until the opening of the 1997 season.

There Joltin' Joe, the greatest living Yankees legend, said, "I've never seen anything like this ticker-tape parade, and I think I've been in a few of them. I want to thank the Yankees for winning this pennant. It brings back fond memories for me.''

There George Steinbrenner said, ''Joe Torre and I have been talking. And our whole team feels that as much as they gave you, you gave much more back to them. You are something special.''

There Joe Torre drew the biggest ovation. After thanking his players and coaches for the effort they had extended, he thanked the fans for their incredible support. ''What energy you showed out there today!'' he exclaimed. ''You could have lit up the whole world today with the energy you put out.''

Torre closed with the best line of all. ''I was wondering why it took me so long to get to a World Series. Forty-two-hundred-plus games, thirty-plus years . . . Well, I guess the good Lord was waiting for me to put on the pinstripes.'' The roar he set off probably carried all the way over to Brooklyn, Joe's old stomping grounds.

When I was young, I had seen images of ticker-tape parades on newsreels that ran before movies started. But even those scenes failed to capture the enormity of such an occasion. As more than one speaker remarked that day, the parade route looked like a sea of humanity.

Every which way you turned your head, you saw people. Happy, joyous, jubilant people. People on the street; people leaning out of office windows; people scrambling up trees, street signs, and stoplights, trying to get a better look at the procession. Sidewalks and storefronts were about the only things you couldn't see. A wall of bodies covered them up.

I kept my remarks at City Hall Plaza brief. "This is the finest city in the world," I said, "and you are the finest fans in the world."

Just to be able to stand there with Joe Torre, our arms raised aloft in triumph, was statement enough for me. What I was feeling at that moment was the same sort of top-of-the-world sensation I'd felt the previous Saturday night at Yankee Stadium. To have been a part of such an extraordinary victory parade was unforgettable. Nothing in three decades in baseball had prepared me for such a rush.

I guess that in years to come, when people ask me about the 1996 victory parade for the Yankees, I'll have to say the same thing that pitcher Kenny Rogers said: "It was unbelievable. You had to see it to believe it."

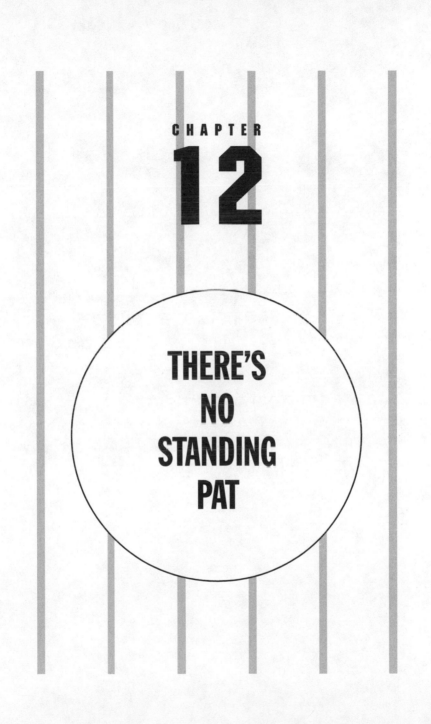

CHAPTER

12

THERE'S NO STANDING PAT

By Wednesday, October 30, as the remnants of the paper avalanche were being swept up off the parade route in Manhattan, and the city's five boroughs had returned to their usual hustle and bustle, we were back in the office working on the composition of the Yankees roster for 1997.

Each of us possessed enough memories from the past ninety-six hours to last a lifetime. But we would have to savor those sweet memories at some later date. The clock was already ticking on the next year. Spring training camp was less than four months away.

It probably goes without saying, but in this era of free agency in baseball, teams will likely undergo major changes between each season. The 1997 Yankees team, for example, will have several significant differences from its predecessor. We'll still be a blend of youth and experience, but some faces will have changed.

We had to get busy right after the parade ended. We had to declare quickly, by November 1 in fact, if we were going to pick up options on several players or let them become unrestricted free agents. Our first move was to renew the options on Darryl Strawberry, Dwight

Gooden, and Charlie Hayes. Each will be back in the new year.

Next, we completed the controversial Graeme Lloyd trade with Milwaukee by receiving infielder Gabby Martinez as the player to be named. Then we added an outfielder from the farm system, Ricky Ledee, to our major-league roster.

After a brief respite, the pace began picking up. We decided to trade catcher Jim Leyritz to California for two minor-league players to be named. In 1997 that move will allow us to have one of our top prospects, Jorge Posada, backing up Joe Girardi. Had we kept Leyritz, whose home run off Mark Wohlers turned around the World Series, we would have impeded Posada's progress. That could have ramifications down the road.

Later in November, we released several players—Mike Aldrete, Tony Fernandez, Melido Perez, Dave Polley, Dave Pavlas, and Brien Taylor—from our forty-man major-league roster. We added outfielder Shane Spencer and pitchers Tim Rumer, Danny Rios, and Rafael Medina. We signed a free-agent pitcher, Julian Vasquez, a right-hander who was receiving rave reviews in the Winter League.

Not surprisingly, in the weeks after the 1996 World Series, free agency began gnawing away at our roster. The same phenomenon has happened to championship teams in other sports—the skimming of talent off the

Dallas Cowboys Super Bowl winning teams comes immediately to mind—principally for two reasons.

One, some of the key contributors to the championship team find themselves very much in demand as free agents and have several offers from which to choose. Two, teams aspiring to reach the next level often sign role players off a championship team, hoping some of the winning aura rubs off on their club.

Starting pitcher Jimmy Key was the first free agent to leave, signing with one of our American League East rivals, Baltimore. We had been talking to Jimmy about a one-year deal with a one-year option, but he preferred the two-year guarantee with the Orioles.

Then John Wetteland, our closer and World Series MVP, signed with the Texas Rangers for $23.9 million. As our play-off series with Texas had demonstrated, the Rangers' one glaring weakness last season was late relief. With the addition of Wetteland, they have armed themselves to prevent such a recurrence in 1997.

As vital a cog as Wetteland was to the Yankees' success in 1996, with 43 saves, we simply couldn't see paying that kind of money for one relief pitcher, especially when we have another great bullpen weapon, Mariano Rivera, to step in and fill the breach.

Rivera will replace Wetteland as our closer in 1997, a progression that reflects one of the major roles of a GM—namely, having someone groomed and ready to step into a critical position. You never want to be caught shorthanded.

The GM, assisted by his scouting department, has to keep one eye directed to the future. GMs are always trying to anticipate needs, looking ahead two or three years to see who might be ready to step in and fill a void. In that sense, a GM making personnel evaluations is like a chess player thinking one or two moves ahead. In baseball, GMs have to think a couple of years ahead.

Let me give you an example. Wade Boggs, one of the premier hitters of his time, is nearing the end of a long and distinguished career. Though I'm sure he'll be our 1997 starter at third base and, if he stays healthy, will enjoy another good year, as GM I have to be evaluating third basemen—either someone from within the organization or free agents—who could play the position for us in 1998 or 1999. That's one reason we renewed the contract of Charlie Hayes and extended him a second option year.

One thing I've learned as a GM is that the future gets here quickly. That explains why the Yankees and other clubs have a sizable investment in developing players in our minor-league system. (In a given year, we'll have about 250 players on seven minor-league teams under contract.) And it is why our scouting program, domestically and internationally, is so extensive. You have to find the talent.

Besides internal development, of course, the other major source of talent is free agency. The impact of free agency can be seen in all professional sports. From Shaquille O'Neal's move from Orlando to Los Angeles in the NBA to the Carolina Panthers and Jacksonville Jaguars in the NFL stockpiling free agents on their rosters (remarkably enough, both second-year NFL franchises advanced to their respective conference championship game), free agency has changed the sports landscape.

The Yankees, for example, were able to retool for the 1996 season with free-agent signings of David Cone, Mariano Duncan, and Kenny Rogers (plus Darryl Strawberry during the summer). Those moves were instrumental in our returning to baseball prominence.

Free agency allows teams with deep pockets to improve their competitiveness in short order. If you have the revenue base, you can transform yourself into a contender almost overnight. Then, if your team develops a winner's attitude and is able to catch a few breaks, it can win a lot of games.

On the other hand, teams in smaller markets, without the same sort of dollars at their command, will find it very difficult to be competitive. There is not a lot you can do besides develop your talent base, do some bottom-fishing in the free-agent pool, and then hope a number of players put together a "career" season.

Because players have so little loyalty to teams—but a

great deal of loyalty to the size of their paychecks—the system of free agency basically allows the rich to get richer. Even so, I believe it's doubtful the "dynasties" in baseball—like the Yankees in the '50s, the Dodgers in the '60s, the Oakland A's in the '70s—will return. Those days when you could keep all the Mantles, Berras, Fords, Howards, Kubeks, and Richardsons together year after year are long gone.

FREE AGENCY SHOCKERS

The kind of player movement that free agency affords may be good for the players, but it's tough on baseball fans. That point was vividly illustrated in December, when we participated in the Roger Clemens sweepstakes. The Yankees were one of the serious bidders for the services of Clemens, who remains one of the best power pitchers in baseball. The veteran Boston right-hander finally signed with the Toronto Blue Jays.

Before free agency arrived, who would have ever thought the Rocket would pitch for any team besides the Red Sox? To imagine anything of the sort would have seemed laughable. Clemens was as synonymous with New England as clam chowder and Stephen King.

Now those kinds of shockers come with the territory.

They are routine. The only big surprise would be if there were a baseball off-season with no shockers.

In December, we signed Joe Girardi, who had solidified our defense and set an outstanding example with his work ethic, to a free-agent contract. He'll get the majority of work in '97 and also serve as Posada's mentor. We also acquired Mike Stanton, a solid left-handed reliever who had been with Texas, through free agency.

Then we filled the hole Jimmy Key left in our starting rotation by signing David Wells, who won 11 games for Baltimore last year. Wells has an outstanding (10-1) lifetime record at Yankee Stadium, a stat we hope he builds on during 1997. I suppose a person could say that our acquiring Wells was a quid pro quo with the Orioles.

On December 20, we decided not to tender contracts to pitcher Scott Kamieniecki and reserve infielder Luis Sojo. In January, we were able to re-sign Sojo to shore up our middle infield, but Kamieniecki signed a free-agent contract with Baltimore.

A NEW YEAR

The new year started on a particularly high note personally, as some friends in Houston helped me pull off a surprise party for Carol. About fifty friends and family, including Keith and Kelley, celebrated her birthday with an elegant dinner at the Ritz-Carlton Hotel.

Slipping something of that magnitude past Carol was like slipping the morning sun past a rooster or a fastball past Hank Aaron, but we managed to pull it off. She seemed thrilled and delighted, and I won't spoil things by saying which birthday it was.

Then, on January 9, 1997, at a black-tie dinner at the Sheraton Boston Hotel, I received the Baseball Executive of the Year award for 1996, presented by the Boston chapter of the Baseball Writers of America. I was proud and flattered that this distinguished group—many of whom I've known since I played with the Red Sox in 1979, and some who raked me over the coals pretty good last summer after the Weathers and Lloyd trades—considered me worthy of recognition. Those guys have plenty of baseball savvy, and they understand the pressures of working in New York and putting together a winner there.

In my remarks, I thanked the baseball writers and told them that my dream of being a baseball GM and being the architect of a world champion had come true. "Believe me, it was only through a lot of perseverance, persistence, and a lot of prayer," I said.

At a news conference before the awards ceremony, I predicted a close race for the American League's Eastern

Division in '97 and said that the Yankees, in making a spirited defense of our crown, aren't going to stand pat.

"I don't think a team should stand pat," I said. "I don't think you can keep a team together for very long these days, anyway, with free agency being the way it is. Guys are gonna change teams, and I don't see anything wrong with that. (That brought a groan from the Beantown press, still smarting over having just lost Clemens to Toronto. But I wasn't being vicious or ugly.)

"I've seen teams that stay with their team too long and wind up having problems. I don't think it's healthy to keep a team together too long. I think you're better off changing a year too soon than waiting a year too late."

I really believe it's critical for a baseball team to bring in one or two young players every year. That gives your club a blend of time-tested experience and youthful exuberance. The main thing is, you don't want your players getting old at the same time.

For example, a portion of the Yankees starting outfield—Paul O'Neill, Darryl Strawberry, and Tim Raines—is beginning to show some age. That's why we plan to bring along Ruben Rivera in 1997, and why in early January we signed switch-hitting outfielder Mark Whiten as a free agent.

A YEAR
AS DEFENDING CHAMPS

In 1997, the Yankees will experience what the Atlanta Braves did in 1996. As defending champions, we will be the king of the hill, the club every other major-league team hopes to supplant. We'll be the prime target to topple.

The '97 Yankees will learn that the most difficult accomplishment in professional sports isn't getting to the top; it's staying there. Many has been the championship team that grew complacent and lost its edge. Many has been the champion that, because of jealousy or envy, fell from within. Many has been the champion that forgot the magic word on which its title was based—*teamwork.* Players on these teams either started putting selfish interests ahead of collective goals, or they sloughed off in their work habits.

AN UNBELIEVABLE START
TO 1997

By the second week of January, after a period of shuttling between Houston and Tampa, I holed up at the Roger Smith Hotel in midtown Manhattan and began preparing for the arbitration process with Bernie Williams, Graeme Lloyd, and David Weathers.

I hoped to avoid arbitration with Lloyd and Weathers but had pretty much decided that we could not avoid it with Williams. We've put an offer of $4.5 million a year on the table for Bernie; but after his performance in the postseason, his agent, Scott Boras, will probably be talking in terms of $6 million. Don't be surprised if we settle in the $5.1 million range. We'll see.

Almost every day that month brought a big development. On Friday, January 10, Dan Gooden died of kidney failure in Tampa. Dan, Dwight's father, was a fine gentleman and a great supporter of his son. After Doc pitched that no-hitter against Seattle at Yankee Stadium last May, he flew to Tampa and gave the ball to Dan, who was scheduled to undergo open-heart surgery the next day. "I did this for you," Dwight told his proud father.

On January 13, we learned that David Wells, who had gone to San Diego for his mother's funeral, had suffered a broken left hand in an altercation. Doctors are hopeful that he'll be healed and ready to go by the opening of spring training or the opening of the 1997 season at the latest. We'll have to wait and see.

At mid-month, legendary golfer Arnold Palmer underwent successful surgery for prostate cancer at the Mayo Clinic. From all reports, the surgery was successful and Palmer will be back leading "Arnie's Army" by this spring. Now we'll have another high-profile spokesman to raise public awareness about the disease, which kills between forty and fifty thousand men each year but which, if detected early, has a nearly 90 percent cure rate.

On January 18, the *New York Times* reported that Joe Torre wanted a contract extension beyond the 1997 season. (We obliged, and on February 21 we extended his contract through the 1999 season. We couldn't let the manager of the world championship team head into a new season on the last year of his contract. I didn't want to go into battle in 1997 without Joe.)

On January 19, I attended funeral services in Tampa for Dan Gooden. Several of us flew down from New York on the Yankees' plane. As if that occasion weren't sad enough for the Goodens, thieves broke into their home and stole a reported $30,000 in possessions while Dwight and his family were at the service.

On January 22, at a ceremony at Yankee Stadium, Don Mattingly announced his retirement from baseball. Don was a great leader for the New York Yankees during his thirteen-year career, including four years as team captain. His enthusiasm and leadership qualities earned him the nickname "Donnie Baseball." Mattingly's jersey number—23—will be retired.

It's a bitter irony for Don that the one year he chose to sit out from baseball was the year the Yankees won their first world championship in eighteen years. Sometimes, life can play cruel tricks on good people.

On January 26, I took a brief break from business and watched Green Bay defeat New England in Super Bowl XXXI. The Packers are another example of a sports team that has improved its talent base through the acquisition of free agents—most prominently, Reggie White. (I highly recommend his autobiography, *In the Trenches*.)

As the end of January approached, I headed into contract negotiations with three players who have three or fewer years of major-league experience. They just happened to be three of our pivotal young stars: Derek Jeter, Andy Pettitte, and Mariano Rivera.

Each of these players made less than $200,000 in 1996. Each of these players will want to make $500,000 or more in 1997. They don't have much leverage in the conversations, but, on the other hand, we don't wish to create any ill will that might affect contract negotiations down the road. We'll have to see how those conversations go.

Overall, in the next few weeks I have to get everyone signed and ready to head to camp in Florida in a positive, upbeat mode. That's the goal of every GM: to put your club together while trying to make everyone happy—and accepting the fact that you can't.

Our payroll for 1996 was $66.1 million. For 1997, it

looks as though it may exceed $70 million. That's laying a lot on the line.

THE 1997 ROSTER

When I look at the Yankees roster headed to Tampa for training camp, I see a strong blend of established veterans and emerging young talent. Is our lineup set? Is our pitching rotation? Ask me today, and I might say they are. Ask me tomorrow, though, and things might have changed.

I've already jotted down a few notes for my speech for the opening of camp on February 22:

First, congratulations on a job well done. You are world champions. You deserve all the accolades. You've earned the respect.

Second, let none of us forget how the Yankees won the pennant in 1996. With teamwork. With a commitment to *we, us, team.*

Third, there's a thin line between .500 teams and .600 teams that play deep into the postseason. The commitment to do all the little things right, to play the game within the game, accounts for the main difference between contenders and pretenders.

Point four, the Yankees in 1997 will again need to

play smart, aggressive baseball—to be the intimidator, not the intimidated.

Five, the New York Yankees never quit. You guys have demonstrated an uncommon brand of mental toughness in being able to ride out tough times and bounce back from adversity. You have a winner's attitude that few major-league teams possess. (I'll remind the players that not many, if any, teams could have come back from a 2-0 deficit by winning three straight in the other guy's house.)

Six, if you guys are willing to work hard and keep your eyes on the prize, you have leaders in Joe Torre, Don Zimmer, Mel Stottlemyre, and the other coaches who can get you back to the Fall Classic.

Finally, I'll say that if they think Yankees fans were excited by the team's first world championship in eighteen years, just wait until we win again in 1997.

"Gentlemen," I will say to them, "in this room are the very people who can become champions of the world again in 1997. If we use the motto *we, us, team*— if we subscribe to it and believe in it wholeheartedly—we will do it again. Believe me, if you make a commitment to one another, *we can repeat!*"

Soon enough, the 1997 baseball season will be here and we'll climb aboard that giant roller coaster of winning streaks, losing streaks, comebacks, rallies, slumps, injuries, trades, waivers, and all the other unexpected complications that arise.

One way or another, I feel confident Bob Watson will make it to the end of another exciting ride. After thirty-two years in baseball—this great game that I love so much—surviving may be the one thing I do best.

APPENDIX

For more information about prostate and other forms of
cancer, please contact

> **The American Cancer Society**
> **1599 Clifton Road N.E.**
> **Atlanta, GA 30329-4251**
> **(800) ACS-2345**
>
> **The National Cancer Institute**
> **(800) 4-CANCER**

ABOUT THE AUTHORS

Bob "Bull" Watson has spent thirty-plus years in baseball, most recently as vice president and general manager of the 1996 World Champion New York Yankees. He became baseball's first African-American GM in 1993.

A two-time all-star selection with the Houston Astros, Watson scored baseball's one-millionth run in 1975. To date he is the only major-leaguer to hit for the cycle in both leagues.

Watson is an advocate for the PSA blood test and early screening for prostate cancer. He and his wife, Carol, reside in Houston and New York.

Russ Pate is a freelance writer and author. He lives in Dallas, Texas, with his wife, Becky. This is his sixth book.